GOD'S BOUNTY:

ON THE GODS AND MEN OF VENEZUELA

PART ONE
OF
THE CHILDREN OF BA'AL

© Henry Williams, 2021

Table of Contents

This book is dedicated to the enduring memory of:

My Grandfather A.H. Williams (1929-2021)
My rock of Gibraltar.

&

The Huguenot Museum in Rochester, Kent, United Kingdom
Your hard work and dedication to archiving our shared identity
has been my inspiration.

God's Bounty
Preface

"The Owl of Minerva spreads its wings only with the falling of the dusk".
G.W.F. Hegel (1820). Elements of the Philosophy of Right

I would like you to picture a real-life Westworld; a beautiful, lush tropical paradise, rich in natural resources and peopled with thinking, feeling humans. As in Michael Crichton's screenplay, the adventurers who arrived there were encouraged to enjoy and exploit their 'new' world, whether they were there to settle or merely plunder its resources. As for the original inhabitants, the indigenous tribes, the Europeans behaved towards them as humans behaved towards the Hosts in Westworld; killing, raping or stealing from them was not treated as a crime but rather a right of conquest.

It is unsurprising, therefore, that in this real life Westworld, where settlers, adventurers and native cultures were forced to mix together, the violence, greed and lust present at the outset would solidify into a foundation of corruption and banal cruelty over the following five hundred years, dividing and destabilising the nation and brutalising its society.

When viewed in this context, the current turmoil is merely the third act of a tragedy. With this in mind and in an attempt to

7

introduce the topic of Venezuela in a way that does not overwhelm the reader, I have structured my book in three parts: 'God's Bounty', 'The Rake's Progress' and, the final volume, 'Paradise Lost'. My hope is that, in clarifying and explaining how Venezuela has become what it is, we can avoid a fourth act of the tragedy; we need to, quite literally, turn over a new leaf and stop making the mistakes of the past and understand the present in order to make the changes needed to shape a better future.

As a British-Venezuelan historian and social scientist of International Affairs, I saw that there was an unexplored rich tapestry to Venezuela's 500-year-old history that I wanted to share with you. Indeed, for those Venezuelans like me who grew up abroad after the rise of Chavez's autocratic regime, Venezuela's history may, like a bad taxidermy, seem messy, incomplete and nonsensical. However, the bones of history still exist and, by stripping away the mistakes and padding applied by ignorance or individuals with vested political interests, a more comprehensive view of Venezuelan culture emerges.

I am thankful to History Professor Matthias Röhrig Assunção, Dr. Martin Idel, Dr. Flor Kent, Peter Hetherington, Caryl Topolski, Lorraine Zuleta, my large and supportive extended family, and wife (and Editor) Sophie, for their patience, guidance, proofreading and encouragement while I write this history book series about my beloved country of Venezuela. Sadly, over the last 20 years Venezuela has entered a race to the bottom, combining complete moral, political and economic decline to become the worst iteration of the country it has ever possibly been, to the detriment of millions of Venezuelan lives. Indeed, Venezuela has arguably become a 'Failed State' with a worthless currency, rampant dollarisation and a crumbling infrastructure despite having access to the abundant natural resource of oil which, as of 2020, has also now plummeted in price in the global commodities markets.

This frighteningly rapid moral, economic, political and societal decline and financial collapse can be traced to the adoption by Venezuela's political elite over the past 20 years of dreadful working practices such as rampant corruption, the theft and expropriation of private property and a mismanagement of public funds. These policies based on a poor grasp of ethics, not to mention a lack of understanding of monetary, financial and economic policy.

However, I believe that to blame the current crisis on the last 20 years is to ignore the last 500 years of Venezuela's written history, which demonstrates how corruption, selfishness and expropriation are behaviours that have been the central pillars of its politics for hundreds of years. The modern-day Bolivarian Revolution, aptly named after the son of a family who made their entire fortune from the misappropriated property of a subjugated native population, was not a Black Swan event, but rather a repetition in a pattern of behaviour, caused by the same attitudes and principles which Chavez and his followers affected to scorn in the elites who they then replaced.

"All animals are equal, but some are more equal than others"
George Orwell, Animal Farm

Indeed, my personal belief is that to achieve the true rebirth and potential of Venezuela's Economy and to allow for the development of green shoots to grow and flourish once more in this bountiful land, this centuries old ethos of militarism, materialism, paternalism, prejudice and strict adherence to elitism and systems of hierarchy will have to finally change. Personally, I believe that this democratic change will only come about through the development of a 'Parliament of the People' that will allow Venezuelans the opportunity to find political representation regardless of where they live or their economic status. At present my work as leader of Venezuela Alternativa has been to provide Venezuelans with the groundwork and necessary support to continue to survive in a living hell.

I began this work as a post-mortem of Venezuela's 'Command Economy' in 2018. It has since evolved into a three-part series and perhaps will grow into much more. I now believe that a historical and archaeological study of Venezuela and its past is a necessary part of its journey towards growth and prosperity, as history serves to demonstrate time and time again that the reason all forms of authoritarianism eventually fail is principally because any economy based on a small handful of actors will eventually find its demise through the sheer entropy that comes from the structure of a monopoly.

Mathematicians use a simple proof to demonstrate this by proving how zero factorial is equal to one. This mathematical proof is known to philosophers as the 'Socratic Paradox'. In other words, it amounts to an understanding that thinking that you know everything fundamentally amounts to actually knowing nothing or as Socrates is said to have put it: "I neither know nor think that I know" (Plato, Apology 21d). This stubborn state of blissful ignorance is also known as the 'Dunning-Kruger effect', a cognitive bias that has been shown to demonstrate why people (or politicians) with a surprisingly lack of ability to perform a task tend to overestimate their ability.

The fall of Communism in Latin America and the end of 'Chavismo' in Venezuela could bring with it an opportunity to rebuild the country in a way that could truly benefit its people and ensure long-term prosperity through anti-corruption initiatives that foster economic stability. Independence, expertise and good governance, rather than political centralism and corruption, are the keys to the development of a well-respected and successful country. The silver lining of hitting rock-bottom is that it exposes the foundations upon which to rebuild anew.

The aim of this volume and the series is to present a comprehensive study of Venezuela's cultural history and politics in order to begin to delineate in a practical manner, through the study of its history and its people, a strategy on how to rebuild Venezuela as a viable ecological, financial and trade driven hub for Latin America. This blueprint will attempt to set new standards in Venezuela by using tried and tested principles, practices and methods from countries around the world determined to have the least corrupt and most successful economies.

I hope that you all enjoy this voyage of discovery with me.

Henry Williams
April 18, 2021

God's Bounty:
On the Gods and Men of Venezuela.

Part One of The Children of Ba'al.

Chapter One

First Principles: Weaving the Threads

"There are today no longer Frenchmen, Germans, Spaniards, Englishmen….; there are only Europeans."
Jean-Jacques Rousseau (1772)

A Game of Life

The idea for this book began in the early 2000s, when the author, inspired by Conway's Game of Life, began to program his own version. In doing so, he learnt about 'recursively enumerable sets', which in simple terms are looping processes, such as a seed which grows into a flower which then produces new seeds that, in turn, produce new flowers.

As suggested in this famous song, "Where have all the flowers gone" by Peter, Paul and Mary, recursive enumeration, "a process in which new things emerge from old things by fixed rules" (Hofstadter 1979: 152), applies as much to the study of social structures as it does to the natural world. Indeed, even Aristotle in his seminal work 'Politics' reasoned that "every state is a community of some kind, and every community is established with a view to some good" (Jowett, 1885: 1).

As a millennial born in a digital age, the author reasoned that if the complex mutations that emerge from Conway's Game of Life are based on simple rules, it may be possible to untangle the legal and social rules of country such as Venezuela and, ultimately, come to understand the first principles from which these rules have been derived, separating the complex web of social structures and history into easily followable threads which we can then use to re-weave a more inclusive tapestry. This chapter has been called 'First Principles: Weaving the Threads' as an homage to the author's Huguenot ancestors, some of whom were silk weavers in London and to emphasise the importance of this first stage of unravelling the woven threads to our journey.

Figure 1: Glider Formations: Conway's Game of Life

Whilst this process may sound daunting, to say the least, the author took great comfort in the fact that other academics have been enjoying considerable success in an analogous field of study, that is the history of language.

After all, societies like languages, are shaped by both the history of the culture and the actions and needs of its people, for example, the editors of a dictionary can attempt to forecast an 'unknown' variable, like the future popularity of 'on fleek', based on 'known' variables, like viewing figures of tv shows, its use in the media, celebrity endorsements and even which fashions are becoming popular, as a rise in the popularity of 'grunge' could spell obscurity for a word associated with the opposite style.

Therefore, it follows that the author could conduct a similar 'factor analysis' to forecast the unknown variables at play in present day Venezuela based on the known variables found in the historical data of its population, in order to derive a better understanding of 'what's hot and what's not', or the fundamentals underlying the 'social topology' of that culture. However, in order to do this successfully, we must first explore the symbols, history, laws, religion of Venezuela and its social structure, separating out the threads so that we can derive a plethora of unobserved underlying factors and first principles that have served to define the Venezuelan people as a unique nation and culture.

The importance of writing a work of this nature are the numerous advances in our understanding of human society, psychology, archaeology, history and anthropology that have come to pass since 1963 thanks to the diligent work of thousands of academics and with a renewed interest in truth, civics, civil society and democracy.

This renewed passion for a greater knowledge on the inner working of our social fabric is especially demonstrated in the recent spike in popularity in films like 'V for Vendetta' and 'The Matrix'; popular tv-shows like 'Westworld', 'Game of Thrones', 'Altered Carbon', and 'The Expanse'; popular serialised works of fiction like 'The Hunger Games series', 'The Complete Harry Potter Collection' and 'A Song of Ice and Fire'; and popular songs like 'Seven Nation Army' by the White Stripes, 'Killing in the Name' and 'Wake up' by the band Rage Against the Machine; all modern works of art that have served to explore an age old political dichotomy that some mainstream journalists say mirror the frustrations that came to a head with the European student protests of 1968.

European Total War and Independence

The author hopes that this historical study may serve as a much-needed foundation to begin to understand Venezuela's 'social topology' and 'civic culture' in a similar manner to Aristotle's 'Politics', Gabriel Almond and Sidney Verba's 1963 work 'The Civic Culture: Political Attitudes and Democracy in Five Nations' and, more recently, Robert Axelrod's computer model that attempted to provide a broad outline of "how cultures and customs are disseminated" (Axelrod 1997: 203).

Axelrod reasoned computationally that convergence was more likely in similar cultures, a similar outlook to that of Jean-Jacques Rousseau in the quote at the start of this chapter, serves to demonstrate that the acceptance of European 'cultural convergence' was understood as early as the 18th Century, even though members of the Aristocracy would argue that 'European' was a concept introduced by Charlemagne the *Pater Europae* (Father of Europe) in as early as the 8th century.

However, going by Rousseau's timeline, we find how a few years after Rousseau writes of European convergence in his essay 'Considerations on the Government of Poland' (1772), the declaration of independence of the American colonies from Britain is written (1776), the declaration of independence of the Latin American colonies from Spain is written (1810) and not to mention the implosion and collapse of the Great Colombia project (1823) into the distinctive territories we know today as Colombia, Ecuador, Panama and Venezuela. This should demonstrate that European cultural convergence and language similitude in practice did not guarantee peace between Europe and the Americas, and neither did it guarantee peace within continental Europe itself.

Moreover, a mere 30 years after Rousseau wrote his observation of European convergence quoted at the start of this chapter, the nations of Europe would be fighting a total war against Napoleon and his allies that would end with Napoleon's defeat at the battle of Waterloo (1815) at the hands of a coalition of British, Hanoverian and Dutch-Belgian troops and serve as the inspiration for the song 'Waterloo' the winning Swedish entry for Eurovision in 1974.

The disintegration of nineteenth century Europe into warring factions arguable started in 'opinion hyperpolarisation', which is where a continent, country or society lacks a cultural and ideological consensus between defined groups of individuals. For example, if three neighbouring countries are all Catholic monarchies in 1500 but, by 1800 they have become a Catholic republic, a Catholic monarchy and a Protestant monarchy, what started out as an ideologically similar group of societies will be divided by religion and politics.

Whilst cultural similarity is no guarantee of peace, the violent and volatile history of France (the Catholic Republic), England (the Protestant monarchy) and Spain (the Catholic monarchy) over the past five hundred years is indicative of the threat 'opinion hyperpolarisation' poses to international harmony and, indeed, its Democratic institutions. Recent studies have sought to develop a "metric to quantify [hyperpolarisation]" (Schweighofer et al, 20202:2), using Weighted Balance Theory (WBT), where a chart was used to demonstrate the divergence in attitudes between the surveyed groups by mapping each group's position using two co-ordinates on an X and Y axis.

The relevance of 'culture dissemination' and 'opinion hyperpolarisation' within the context of a defined European culture and history to a study of a Latin American country like Venezuela should not be underestimated. The history of the four main ethnicities which make up Venezuela will be considered in detail by the author later, however, for the purpose of this chapter, it suffices to say that, immediately following the Spanish conquest in 1492, there were two main groups, which could broadly be described as the pre-Columbian indigenous cultures and the Spanish conquistadors. Later, the Spanish brought in a third group, enslaved Africans, and a fourth group emerged, the mixed race 'typical' Venezuelan, who is descended from European, indigenous and African forebears. However, the dominant political forces and cultural influences thrust upon the American continent and its indigenous peoples have been European. This is primarily due to the fact that, firstly, from 1492 onwards, the pre-Columbian native indigenous cultures were either destroyed, assimilated or pushed to the territorial fringes of modern-day Venezuela by the Spanish conquest. Secondly, under both the Spanish Crown and the later republic established by Spanish descended 'revolutionary' Simon Bolivar, the ruling classes of Venezuela have traced their ancestors to Europe.

The Cultural Similitudes

It was the cultural similitudes of Venezuela with his native Britain that led the author's father in 1985 to begin a detailed set of journals about Venezuela and its people which spanned a period of over ten years of written history. Using his journals and amalgamating his observations with an understanding of the history, language and culture of Venezuela's people, the author hopes to be able to include the detail of his father's observations and first-hand account of that period, as part of a work of its own, to add further depth and a different angle to this comprehensive study of Venezuela's people.

Moreover, to begin to derive the building blocks of any society, we can also look to the institution of the United Nations, specifically the Universal Declaration of Human Rights (UDHR) since according to the UDHR "the family is the basic unit of society". To sociologist Robert K. Merton, the 'family' is understood to operate within a social structure and sociologist John Levi Martin theorised that "macro-scale structures are the emergent properties of micro scale cultural institutions" (Freeman 2019: 112), which is perhaps why many monarchs have historically styled themselves as the 'father' or 'mother' to their nations, thereby hoping to evoke not only obedience in their subjects but also love and loyalty.

Harkening back to the beginning of this chapter, we could also consider society to be analogous to another macro structure, a language, which made of three microstructures; an alphabet, the words formed of the letters in that alphabet and the set of grammatical rules which orders those words into intelligible sentences.

Considering the macro and microstructures in the above contexts, we can then begin to derive a hypothesis that asks:

To what extent do cultural institutions influence the morphological changes in the long-term development of a culture and its social fabric?

With this hypothesis at its core, it may be theoretically possible to begin to construct a historical study that advances our ethnographical understanding of Venezuela, which is comprehensive enough to be used as a framework to explore the history and cultures created and developed by the relationships between these micro-scale 'human engines' and thus perhaps begin to answer the more complex political questions about the rule of Law, Democracy and economics of Terra Firma, with specific focus on the peoples of modern day Venezuela.

In this context, what is meant by ethnographic research is a study that uses a qualitative method where researchers observe and/or interact with a study's participants in their real-life environment. Due to the mainly historical nature of this study, we will be using archaeological evidence, historical documents and written/videotaped observations and interactions, some of which includes quantitative information, such as statistics.

European Settlers

At this early point in this series of books, it is crucial to note that the early European settlers are one of the key human engines to begin with in order to unlock and therefore understand the current complexities inherent in modern Venezuelan society and its current social and political crisis. However, that is not to say that the current tragedy is in any way Europe's fault, which would be rather absurd, but to come to terms with the sequence of events that led to and began in 1492 and ended with the creation of Venezuela in its present form.

In fact, the 'Catalogo de pasajeros a Indias' (West Indies passenger records) from the 16th century suggest that the "conquerors of the territory of present-day...Venezuela were unusual in that they featured a higher proportion of Castilians than of Andalusians and Extremeños" (Boyd-Bowman 1973: 31) than any other province in the New World. Moreover, from 1579 to 1600, 80% of the settlers who arrived at the Province of Terra Firma, which encompassed both modern day Colombia and Venezuela, were from Southern Spain, 60% of which were from Seville (Boyd-Bowman 1976: 88). The author will be discussing the effect of this in a future chapter.

Once it becomes clear that the early European settlers of 'Terra Firma' (English: dry land) were predominantly of Andalusian origin, the fact that they named the Province founded in 1533 'New Andalucía', a territory in which we currently find the country's present capital of Caracas, perhaps should come as no surprise to the reader, especially due to its lack in originality.

Moreover, alongside these settlers we find 'adventurers' described as "Dutch and German" (Salmon 1746: 263) and find evidence within the passenger records from 1534 of Spanish settlers to Terra Firma stating they have arrived "con los alemanes" (Boyd-Bowman 1973: 32) with the Germans. Moreover, in this group of Europeans we find a decree for horse riders (Spanish: Jinetes) from the province of Granada to accompany Colombus on his second trip (A.G.I, 1493).

This would seem a rather strange statement to encounter until we uncover that in its earliest written history, the polity of Venezuela is referred to as *Klein-Venedig* (Little Venice) by its German Governor Nikolaus Federmann (Roth, 2017: 439) in his book *Indianische Historia* (Indian History) published in 1557, when it was a domain granted to the Welser family of Augsburg in 1528 by Holy Roman Emperor Charles V (Charles I of Spain). This move, further explored later in the book, is seen by some historians as an effort to settle the debts the monarch had built up with the Welser Bank, an accounting practice observed at the time as "counting unpaid loan balances as fictive advances in a new contract" (Tracy, 2002: 309) and by other historians as simply the traditional practices of Spanish Kings to their vassals (Friede 1961: 135).

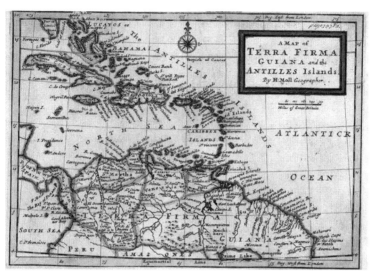

Figure 2: A Map Of Terra Firma by H. Moll from
Salmon, T. (1746), Modern History: or the Present State of All Nations Volume III

Nevertheless, it is undeniable that in Venezuela's recent history Venezuelan authors like Laureano Vallenilla Lanz who wrote *Democratic Caesarism* (1919) sought to repurpose 19th century Euro-American racial theory narratives of "'blood' or biology determining other non-biological qualities" (Wade 2019: 11) to promote racial stereotypes defined in the Spanish *casta* (caste) paintings that first appeared in the 18th Century and became popular under the first Bourbon monarch of Spain, Phillip V (1700-46).

The Cultures of Terra Firma

This study will also seek to deconstruct these narratives and demonstrate that that Venezuelan culture was not created in a vacuum, or spontaneously emerged ex nihilo *fit* (made from nothing) and is not strictly of Spanish origin (whatever *that* even means!), but that it is quantifiably Castilian, Andalusian, German, native American and African in its composition. Moreover, it is this delightful complexity in the interactions between the various cultural engines which makes Venezuela such an interesting place to study and write a book about.

Indeed, aside from the Europeans we find evidence of the communities of Native American tribes that, according to radiocarbon dating, inhabited Venezuela from about 14,000 BCE These complex pre-Columbian civilizations will be discussed in the next chapter. Another particularly important aspect that requires discussion will be the cultural influence of slavery, which will be introduced in the next chapter and expanded upon throughout this book in order to provide a comprehensive view of the African influence on the Venezuelan people and its culture.

Bibliography

A.G.I., (23 May 1493). Patronato 9, fols. 4 rto. Barcelona, Real Cédula a Hernando de Zafra.

Almond, G. A., & Verba, S. (1989). The Civic Culture: Political Attitudes and Democracy in Five Nations. SAGE.

Axelrod, R. (1997). 'The dissemination of culture', *Journal of Conflict Resolution* **41**, pp. 203-26
Boyd-Bowman, P. (1973), Patterns of Spanish Emigration to the New World (1493-1580)

Boyd-Bowman, P. (1976). 'Patterns of Spanish Emigration to the Indies until 1600', *The Hispanic American Historical Review* **56** (4), pp. 580-604

Boyd-Bowman, P. (1976). 'Patterns of Spanish Emigration to the Indies 1579-1600', *The Americas*
33 (1), pp. 78-95, P.88 Andalusian (1579-1600) Province of Tierra Firma:

Federmann, N. (1557) Indianische Historia. Ein schöne kurtzweilige Historia Niclaus Federmanns des Jüngern von Ulm erster raise so er von Hispania und Andolosia auss in Indias des Occeanischen Mörs gechan hat, und was ihm allda ist begegnet biss auff sein widerkunfft inn Hispaniam, auffs kurtzest beschriben, gantz lustig zu lesen. Hagenau: Sigmund Bund.

Freeman, O. (2019). Invitation to Sociology: A Humanistic Perspective. Scientific e-Resources. Chapter 12

Friede, J. (1961). Los Welser En La Conquista De Venezuela. Caracas: Ediciones Edime

Hofstadter, D. R. (1979). Gödel, Escher, Bach: an eternal golden braid (Vol. 13). New York: Basic books.

Jowett, B. (Ed.). (1885). The Politics of Aristotle: Introduction and translation. Vol. 1. Clarendon Press.

Lawley, D., & Maxwell, A. (1962). Factor Analysis as a Statistical Method. Journal of the Royal Statistical Society. Series D (The Statistician), 12(3), 209-229. doi:10.2307/2986915

Mendisco, F., Pemonge, M. H., Leblay, E., Romon, T., Richard, G., Courtaud, P., & Deguilloux, M. F. (2015). Where are the Caribs? Ancient DNA from ceramic period human remains in the Lesser Antilles. Philosophical transactions of the Royal Society of London. Series B, Biological sciences, 370(1660), 20130388.

Roth, J. (2017) Sugar and slaves: The Augsburg Welser as conquerors of America and colonial foundational myths, Atlantic Studies, 14:4, 436-456, DOI: 10.1080/14788810.2017.1365279

Rouse, I., (1992) The Tainos: Rise and Decline of the People Who Greeted Columbus, New Haven & London: Yale University Press.

Rousseau, J.J., (1772) 'Considerations on the Government of Poland'. In Vaughan (ed.), (1915). *The Political Writings of Jean Jacques Rousseau*, Volume II, Cambridge: Cambridge University Press.

Salmon, T. (1746), Modern History: or the Present State of All Nations Volume III, London: Thomas Wotton, pp. 240-63.

Schweighofer, S., Schweitzer, F., & Garcia, D. (2020). A Weighted Balance Model of Opinion Hyperpolarization, Journal of Artificial Societies and Social Simulation, 131, 469.

Tracy, J. D. (2002). Emperor Charles V, impresario of war: campaign strategy, international finance, and domestic politics. Cambridge: Cambridge University Press.

Wade, P., Scorer, J., & Aguiló, I. (2019). Cultures of Anti-Racism in Latin America and the Caribbean.

Chapter Two

The Maize of the Taino

"Another World, another nation; All men shall then discovered see".

Seneca, Tragedy of Medea, Act II circa 50 CE

A Clash of Civilizations

The author recalls very clearly how the animated film *Titan A.E.* (2000) was in cinemas in Venezuela while Hugo Chavez came to power and began flexing his political muscles. The sci-fi film explores the theme of the aftermath of a conquered people and the complete destruction of their home but not their culture, in very much the same way as the Biblical account of the destruction of Jerusalem in 587 BCE at the hands of the Babylonian king Nebuchadnezzar II. The story seemed to me to mirror what was to come in Venezuela, an allegory of the exodus of Venezuelans abroad that would inevitably occur once Chavismo had destroyed their country.

However, despite Chavismo's efforts, under the ironically named 'Great Leap Forward' project, to mutate Venezuelan society, its politics and institutions into a mirror of the Cuban authoritarian model, resulting in the unrecognizable failed state we see today, the Venezuelan Nation and its civil society has survived, albeit outside of its native land. The mass exodus of Venezuelans escaping the crisis to other countries, has meant that every individual or family group has taken with them the customs, culture, history, language and culinary delights of Venezuela with them, meaning Venezuela is kept alive by the network of families and friends who remember it. Therefore, can there such a thing as the death of a Nation while there are still those who remember it and are taught to celebrate and cherish its customs?

That question may have been unexpectedly explored by the politician Ken Livingstone in a Guardian article published in August 2017 under the title *Ken Livingstone: Venezuela crisis due to Chávez's failure to kill oligarchs.* Indeed, the article quotes the former London Mayor Ken Livingstone with saying on Talk Radio that "One of the things that Chávez did when he came to power, he didn't kill all the oligarchs. There was about 200 families who controlled about 80% of the wealth in Venezuela," (Elgot, 2017). A reminder that mass-murder and the fate of execution enacted upon Romanov men, women and children and their entourage by the Bolsheviks in 1918-1919 was still being seen by some as a conceivable political strategy even in the 21st Century.

However, this reasoning that mass-murder would suddenly change the culture of Venezuela is faulty as well as completely immoral. Venezuela at the turn of the last century was somewhat different to Tsarist Russia. To completely expunge Venezuela of its democratic ideals, culture and institutions, Ken Livingstone's figure of 200 families expressed on Talk Radio was out by at least a factor of 50,000. Moreover, to eradicate over 10 million households in an overt and violent manner is a genocide that is

31

historically ascribed to the fall of Carthage to Rome, whereby "Buildings and walls were raised to the ground; the plough passed over the site, and salt was sown in the furrows made" (Ridley, 1986: 144), which would simply have served to raise unwanted attention from the international community onto an increasingly brutal authoritarian regime.

Pre-Columbian America

The story of the Amazon is believed to have begun with a cataclysmic event, a meteor strike near the Yucatan peninsula, around 66 million years ago, that completely obliterated the surrounding pre-existing ecosystem, the ash that settled on the ground perhaps served to fertilise the soil and allowed fast growing angiosperms to dominate and develop into the densely packed rainforest canopy that still dominates northern south America (Carvalho et al., 2021: 63) to this day. From the ashes of destruction came new life and a biodiversity unparalleled elsewhere in the world.

Much like the slow burn catastrophe that is occurring in present-day Venezuela, in 1492, we had the start of another cataclysmic event that would drastically change the course of the Americas and its native peoples. As discussed in the previous chapter, that "no culture appears out of a void" (Sanoja, 1965: 232), in this chapter we discuss that this also applies to the pre-Columbian native American cultures of South America and the Caribbean that will be discussed in this chapter.

Nevertheless, the modern widely held belief amongst the general public is that when Christopher Columbus arrived at the New World, he encountered a *terrae nullius* (English: nobody's land) populated by a less technologically advanced and homogeneous people whom according to Bartolomeo Las Casas, *Historia de Las Indias*: "en todas estas islas hablaban una sola lengua" (English: in all these islands they spoke the same language) (De Las Casas, 1875:I:326), not strictly true, but we will discuss the linguistic similarities between the tribes later on in this chapter.

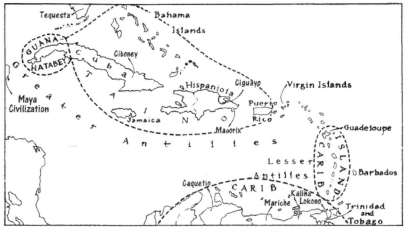

Figure 3: Map of Pre-Columbian Settlements

European sources written at the time and archaeological studies carried out since, demonstrate that the reality was somewhat more complex than Las Casas would lead us to believe. Indeed, during his multiple voyages Columbus kept diaries that meticulously detailed his multiple introductions to a very ancient, culturally defined and technically advanced set of communities whose own journey into America is currently believed to have been underway by 35,000 BCE according to the radiocarbon dating of Palaeolithic artefacts found near Lewisville, Texas (Crook and Harris, 1957).

This journey into the continent of America, currently understood to have begun at the Beringian Land Bridge crossing which served to link Eurasia with North America, continues into South America, where we find remnants of a human culture dating back from 14,000 BCE in the north-western part of modern-day Falcon state, Venezuela in a place called Taima-Taima.

As far back as 1590 a Spanish Jesuit cleric by the name of Jose de Acosta began to theorise that Native Americans were descended from an ancient nomadic people who had followed game animals over a hypothetical land bridge from Asia into America (Acosta 1604: 57). His book 'The Natural and Moral History of the Indies' details his theories and thoughts about the indigenous people the Europeans first encountered in the Americas.

De Acosta even goes as far as to state that "the ancients had some knowledge of the new world" (Acosta, 1604: 33) based on his reading and understanding of Hanno the Carthaginian Navigator's routes in Pliny the Elder's *Natural History* (Bostock and Riley, 1855: 2.67). A navigation route of mythical significance[1] that described the way to ἠλύσιον πεδίον[2] (the Elysian Fields) known

---

[1] An earthly paradise believed by the Ancient Greeks to be inhabited by the heroes of Greek mythology.

also as the 'Fortunate Islands' which according to Acosta was subsequently banned by the Carthaginian Senate lest "with the desire of new lands they should leave to love their own Country" (Acosta, 1604: 33).

This theory, has been recently expanded upon by Lucio Russo in 2014, in his work *L'America dimenticata*, in which he proposes that due to the ancient knowledge lost with the fire at the Great Library of Alexandra in Egypt in 48 BCE during the Great Roman Civil War fought by Julius Caesar, this loss may have had the knock on effect of reducing the accuracy of world maps formerly calculated fairly accurately using the circumference method devised by Eratosthenes of Cyrene, who used the 'Fortunate Islands' as the furthest western point.

Russo believes that later inaccuracies found in maps at the time of Greek mathematician and geographer Ptolemy may be due to the fact that the 'Fortunate Islands' may have been mistakenly thought to have been in the location of the Canary Islands off the west coast of the Iberian Peninsula, rather than the Lesser Antilles. Indeed, a fascinating theory that attempts to shed a light

---

[2] It may be of interest to note that 'the Elysian Fields' or 'le Champs-Élysées' has come to represent in Modern French a long, wide, beautiful and verdant avenue in Paris lined with trees at either side that runs between the Arc de Triomphe to the west and the Place de la Concorde to the East, forming part of the *Voie Triomphale* or *Voie Royale* designed and created in the 17th century during the reign of the 'Sun King' Louis XIV and oriented on a 26 degree angle to follow the course of the Sun, rising in the east and setting in the west.

and provide a new perspective on trans-Atlantic travel during the ancient world, and as we will touch upon in a later chapter, when it comes to mapping the New World cartographical errors can still be seen to occur and be reproduced even in more recent times.

Moreover, the legend of the Fortunate Isles may have also led self-published author Gunnar Thompson to attempt to link Ancient Mediterranean cultures with the Taino Amerindian culture by confusing Pliny's 'black millet' or 'Indian wheat' described as having a "large grain and reed like stalk growing to seven feet" (Spiller, 2012: 38) introduced into the Mediterranean diet around 67-77 A.D with the Taino's crop *ma-his* (maize). Therefore, it is clear that that the lands of the Saladoid, who are now more commonly associated with the Arawak tribes inhabiting the South American mainland and divided into the distinct Taino and Kalinago (Island Caribs) communities inhabiting the Antilles, had served and continue to inspire the imaginations of European scholars.

Indeed, the "timid Tainos" (Davidson, 1997: 255) Columbus encountered on the island of Hispaniola spoke to him of the "man-eating Caribs" (Davidson 1997: 255). A rumour which gives us the root of our shared European word cannibal, which comes from *Caniba*, the name Colombus transcribed for the Island Caribs or Kalinago inhabiting the Lower Antilles.

Fortunately, these two Caribbean cultures have survived to the present day. Eugene Jarecki's documentary the *Quest of the Carib Canoe* (1999) about a sea voyage that took place from the Lower

Antilles to Venezuela by modern day descendants of the Kalinago (Island Caribs) demonstrates a people seeking to trace the migratory route taken by their ancestors back to their place of origin and set the record straight about the rumours surrounding a strong sea faring people over five-hundred years later.

In the same manner, in modern day Puerto Rico we still find a proud Taino culture where according to the National Geographic's Genographic project, 60% of the population of Puerto Rico is carrying the maternal lineage of the Taino genome. It must also be noted that the Taino paternal lineages were not carried by any of the Puerto Rican men, 80% of whom were found to be carrying the paternal lineages of the European genome. In simple terms, this indicates a genocide of the male half of the indigenous population, with the female population being taken as either slaves or wives which, in the sixteenth, seventeenth and eighteenth centuries, were slaves in all but name. The author will be going into the history of slavery in the Americas in more detail later on in the book.

Indeed, as shown in the map at the beginning of this chapter, the settlements Columbus encountered were not part of a monoculture but can be described in terms of four distinct general groupings based on a shared language, culture and tools between the tribes. The Guanahatabey[3], Taino, Caribs and Island

---

[3] Guanahatabey: the Taino interpreter for Columbus could not communicate with them (Rouse, 1992: 20-21)

Caribs. However, because the focus of this study is on the cultures that have influenced Venezuela, we will maintain focus on the Caribs of which the island Caribs are a sub-set and the Taino whose migratory ancestors we will describe as the Saladoid.

What remains of the original Saladoid culture, which according to archaeological evidence spanned the Antilles and mainland Venezuela, is the remnants of their detailed earthenware pottery, precious items of jewellery and a culture and traditions that are still practiced by some of the inhabitants of the island of Puerto Rico to this day. Moreover, it was believed that no human settlements had existed in mainland South America prior to the early Saladoid settlements that have been dated to 6,000 BCE (Mendisco et al., 2015: 1). This assumption upheld by a North American artefact called a 'Clovis' spearpoint, pre-supposed that any south American settlement would invariably be chronologically post-Clovis.

This would change in 1961 after Venezuelan Archaeologist Jose Maria Cruxent began an excavation of the Taima-Taima archaeological site, which would provide evidence that would put into question the assumptions held at the time about Paleo-American migrations into South America. Indeed, what Cruxent uncovered in the north-west region of Venezuela in Taima-Taima was archaeological evidence that a pre-Clovis settlement had existed in Venezuela around 12,000 years ago.

The evidence Cruxent would present would be the 'Jobo' "man-made spearpoints... found embedded within the skeletons of extinct [fauna]" (Fiedel, 2000: 40) of the Pleistocene era. One specific example currently on display to the public at the Taima-Taima site is a preserved stone 'Jobo' spearpoint found in the fossilised pelvis of a Mastodon (Woolly Mammoth), numbered in figure 4 below as exhibit 2.

This United Nations Educational, Scientific and Cultural Organization (UNESCO) World Heritage site, now famous for its artefacts that date to the Pleistocene era around 14,000 years ago was the first of its kind and remains the oldest archaeological site uncovered on the Venezuelan mainland and of comparative importance with the cave paintings at Lascaux as they both provide us a window into the behaviours of theses Palaeolithic hunter-gatherers that migrated to South America during the last Ice Age.

From this evidence of Palaeolithic man in Venezuela we encounter a hiatus in archaeological finds through the Meso-Indian period until we encounter the human remains and pre-ceramic artefacts of an early Saladoid civilization in the Banwari site of south western Trinidad dated from about 6,000 BC.E. from "the first migrants to arrive in the region" (Mendisco et al., 2015: 1).

These sophisticated settlements, the result of migrations, are believed to have had two possible origins from the Yucatán Peninsula in the southern region of modern Mexico, a territory that would later become part of the Mayan Empire by the Archaic culture (Casimiroid series) or from the Andean region in western South America the Saladoid culture (Ortoiroid series), specifically an area from the coast of modern day Ecuador to modern day Panama, a territory that would later be dominated by the short lived Inca Empire.

Figure 4: Taima-Taima Paleontological Park exhibit: 1. Tusk of Mammut Americanum (Mastodon); 2. Pelvis of Mastodon with Jobo Spear Point; 3. Tibia of Mastodon; 4. Glyptodont Fossil (Giant Armadillo); 5. Fossilised Cranium of Megatherium (Giant Ground Sloth).

Studies have shown that two distinct civilizations "defined largely on the basis of the different tool types" (Keegan, 1994: 268) the distinct communities had used emerged in the Caribbean, a Casimiroid culture that may have "evolved through continuous ties with Central America" (Keegan, 2015: 48), which might mean that the Casimiroid "ground-stone tools and cultigens...arrived in the islands through exchange" (Keegan, 2015: 48).

Alongside this likely Casimiroid migration from the west we encounter archaeological evidence of "the arrival of the migrating horticulturalists and ceramic-making Saladoid groups into the Lesser Antilles and northeast Greater Antilles beginning around 800 B.C." (Reid, 2018: 237). Nevertheless, based on archaeological evidence found at the Banwari site in Trinidad and Tobago, the Saladoid civilization is also believed to have emerged from "the first migrants to arrive in the region approximately 6000 B.C." (Mendisco et al., 2015: 1).

The Saladoid communities, based on current archaeological evidence of their technology are believed to have a common origin in the Orinoco basin. A holistic picture of the numerous archaeological finds in the area has meant that academics have been able to trace their migration north, from the Orinoco basin, then into the Antilles until reaching the island of Puerto Rico. Indeed, the artefacts associated with the Ortoiroid series have been grinding pebbles and grinding bases. These flour-making and bountiful civilizations may have fostered territorial expansion, exploration and migration, which was followed by an Andean a second wave migration of the Kalinago or Island Caribs, shortly before the arrival of Columbus.

These likely offshoots of a pre-cursor civilization to the Chané settlements at the foothills of the Andes with easy access to the natural canal system of the Amazon basin, would explain why *uné* (water) is a common word amongst all Arawakan languages across South America and the Caribbean as the rivers were the highways that united all the cultures with one another. This unique use of a natural wonder may have inspired the Dutch to build their system of artificial waterways beginning with Amsterdam's

Grachtengordel (the Canal Belt) from 1585 and their series of flat-bottomed canal boats perhaps inspired by the design of the humble narrow boat, the canoe.

Moreover, the use of the Amazon's natural canal system for trade between settlements can also be used to explain the proliferation of Arawak dialects across south America as shown on figure 5, but also demonstrate how the avocado, which was abundant in many sites along the north-central coast of Peru from circa 4450-3750 B.C. and present in Colombia circa 3270 B.C. found its way to Puerto Rico.

Indeed, it has been documented in a study of corn, cassava and yam food starches left on ancient grinding pebbles that the cultigens may, had been introduced by Saladoid immigrants to the islands from approximately 2500 B.C. (Bel, Knippenberg & Pagán-Jiménez, 2018: 391). In addition to this, the presence of these three cultigens combined with the use of grinding pebbles and bases to make them into flour, as well as certain growing and cooking processes in pre-Arawak archaeological sites in de Puerto Rico, Vieques and the Dominican Republic that share similarities with to those observed in Panama and Colombia, may also indicate a distinct type of Casimiroid population migration from the Colombian isthmus to the Greater Antilles.

Taino loan words like 'Hammock' (*hamaca*) (Davidson 1997: 338), 'Maize' (*ma-his*), 'Savannah' (*zavana*), 'Mangrove' (*mangle*), 'Guava' (*guayaba*), 'Papaya' (*papáia*), 'Potato' (batata), 'Cassava' (*casaba*), 'Cigar' (sik'ar), 'Tobacco' (*tambaku*[4]) and 'Hurricane' from the Maya Creator Deity and Storm God *Hu-racan* (one leg) described in the Popol Vuh, were used by the Caribbean communities Columbus encountered in his voyages, words that in themselves can serve to show the blending of the sophisticated agrarian Yucatan and Andean cultures in the Taino people. Moreover, the Arawak words *kanowa* (canoe), *barbacoa* (barbecue), *iwana* (iguana), *manáti* (manatee), *acayouman* (caiman), while they describe a more nomadic river people, they can also serve to demonstrate how necessary it was for Europeans to adopt local words that are still in use to this day to describe the new paradigm they encountered.

Making false assumptions about foodstuffs in an ever changing and evolving social context is a particularly myopic human error. We have a tendency to presume that what we eat today is nature's bounty and was just as easily available to our ancestors; we have all read a book or seen a show which, despite its medieval setting, features potatoes, chocolate or tomatoes; indeed whenever we see the nickname "carrots" used for famous redheads, like Henry VIII or his daughter Elizabeth I, we do not immediately question it, even if we know that the now familiar orange hue of carrots was only developed, through intensive selective breeding in the 17th century under the reign of William

---

[4] Tambaku was "the native name for a peculiarly forked hollow reed, in shape resembling the letter Y" that was used by the Taino to smoke dried Tobacco leaves (Writers of Eminence, 1880: 934).

of Orange. Earlier monarchs like Henry VIII and Elizabeth I only knew carrots as the purple, yellow or white of the wild varieties.

Figure 5: Arawakan Languages in South America.
Light Grey - Northern Arawakan; Dark Grey - Southern Arawakan

Just as carrots were genetically engineered through years of laborious scientific process, the 'bounty' of the Americas was anything but 'natural' or 'god given'; maize, avocados, potatoes, tobacco, chewing gum and chilli peppers were developed by generations of horticulturalists, selectively breeding for higher yields, better flavour, and diversity for at least "7000 years" (Bosland 1996: 479). Moreover, research by Edmar de Oliveira into the Amazon's 'Terra Preta de Indio' otherwise known as

44

anthropogenically made Amazonian Dark Earths (ADE) soils were formed by pre-Columbian settlements who through "crop cultivation and agroforestry altered the modern composition" (De Oliveira et al, 2000: 2) of the soil. A knock-on effect of these soil changes is an increase in biodiversity.

Yet they are easily taken for granted as manna from heaven rather than man-made produce requiring considerable skill, scientific knowledge and time to develop. When you compare the superfood sweetcorn to the wild grasses from which the Saladoid bred it and understand that this crop was so effective that it provided enough of a surplus to mean that, instead of everyone subsistence farming, a small percentage of the population could grow enough food to feed the rest, freeing up the scientists, architects, builders, musicians, artisans and engineers and allowing cultures like the Incas, Aztecs and Mayans to thrive into complex imperial bureaucracies.

The development of sweetcorn and sweet potatoes is arguably more impressive than equally engineered technologies like firearms; a society might be protected by muskets, but it would be exceedingly difficult to argue that handguns serve to build societies like sweetcorn has done, especially when we take into account that famine amongst the poor was common right into the nineteenth century in Europe. Indeed, following the Great Kyoho Famine of 1732, Aoki Konyo, known as Professor Sweet Potato, introduced the idea that large-scale farming of sweet potatoes would avert another famine in Japan. From the first crop harvested in 1735, farms in central and northern Japan have grown an abundance of sweet potatoes that has helped save the Japanese from starvation.

Therefore, the cultural differences between these civilizations and those from Europe seem to be that the Incas, Mayans and Aztecs had defined Imperial bureaucracies that spanned vast territories in central and South America, while Europe was (and remains to this day, even under the auspices of the European Union) a collection of rival nations that have stood quite close together. We can therefore expand upon the 'Needham question' proposed by Joseph Needham about the effect of a stable Chinese Imperial Bureaucracy and utilize his conclusion to argue that European advantage in 1492 came from a place of conflict and competition, specifically in the form of arms races. This may have fostered the development and use of more devastating technologies for use in warfare in the pursuit of an advantage.

Thus, the European military advances developed for one political sphere of influence led to its use in another and the eventual military occupation of the Americas and the real-life Westworld described at the start of this book and which will be expanded upon in later chapters. The indigenous communities did not stand a chance against the newcomers who claimed colonial rights over the Province which they called Terra Firma and turned the Caribbean into the gateway to the land of 'do-as-you-please'. The pestilence, violence and enslavement that would be the defining characteristics of a military invasion that has lasted over five-hundred years.

Nevertheless, there are indigenous communities that have managed to survive to this day, such as the Pemon, Yanomami, Yukpa and Wayuu despite the greed, germs, guns and religion imported to the paradise that was Venezuela by European settlers. My own family which descends from an indigenous tribe called the Caiquetio had their homes at the epicentre of what was to come and built the stilt houses on Lake Maracaibo that gave Venezuela its name "Little Venice" (Roth, 2017: 439). And so, it came to pass that paradise was not only lost but destroyed and industrialised in the search for the accumulation of shiny metal trinkets that cannot feed and sustain like the golden maise and sweet potatoes.

Bibliography

Antczak, A., Urbani, B., & Antczak, M. M. (2017). Re-thinking the Migration of Cariban-Speakers from the Middle Orinoco River to North-Central Venezuela (AD 800). Journal of World Prehistory, 30(2), 131-175. https://link.springer.com/article/10.1007/s10963-017-9102-y

Atkinson, L. G. (Ed.). (2006). The earliest inhabitants: The dynamics of the Jamaican Taino. University of West Indies Press.

Bel M, van den, Knippenberg S., Pagán-Jiménez J.R. (2018). From cooking pits to cooking pots. Changing modes of food processing during the Late Archaic Age in French Guiana. In: Reid BA (ed) The

Archaeology of Caribbean and Circum-Caribbean Farmers (6000 BC-AD 1500). London and New York: Routledge, pp. 391-418.

Bosland, P.W. (1996). Capsicums: Innovative uses of an ancient crop. p. 479-487. In: J. Janick (ed.), Progress in new crops. ASHS Press, Arlington, VA.

Bostock, J., & Riley, H. T. (1855). Pliny the Elder: The Natural History. London. Taylor and Francis, Red Lion Court, Fleet Street.

Carvalho, M.R. et al. (02 Apr 2021) 'Extinction at the end-Cretaceous and the origin of modern Neotropical rainforests', Science: Vol. 372, Issue 6537, pp. 63-68

Crook, W. W., & Harris, R. K. (1957). Hearths and Artifacts of Early Man Near Lewisville, Texas, and Associated Fauna Material.

Davidson, M. H. (1997). Columbus then and now: a life re-examined. University of Oklahoma Press.

De Acosta, J. (1880). The Natural and Moral History of the Indies, trans. Edward Grimston (1604).

De Las Casas, B. (1877). Historia de las Indias (Vol. 1). Imprenta y litografia de I. Paz.

De Oliveira, E. A., Marimon-Junior, B. H., Marimon, B. S., Iriarte, J., Morandi, P. S., Maezumi, S. Y., ... & Feldpausch, T. R. (2020)

Legacy of Amazonian Dark Earth soils on forest structure and species composition. Global Ecology and Biogeography.

Elgot, J. (2017, August 3). Ken Livingstone: Venezuela crisis due to Chávez's failure to kill oligarchs. The Guardian, https://www.theguardian.com/politics/2017/aug/03/ken-livingstone-venezuela-crisis-hugo-chavez-oligarchs

Fiedel, S. J. (2000). The peopling of the New World: present evidence, new theories, and future directions. Journal of Archaeological Research, 8(1), 39-103.

Fitzpatrick, S. M., Carstensen, J. A., Marsaglia, K. M., Descantes, C., Glascock, M. D., Kaye, Q., ... & Technics, I. T. S. (2008). Preliminary petrographic and chemical analyses of prehistoric ceramics from Carriacou, West Indies. Journal of Caribbean Archaeology, 8(2), 59-83.

Fitzpatrick, S. M. (2015). The Pre-Columbian Caribbean: Colonization, population dispersal, and island adaptations. PaleoAmerica, 1(4), 305-331.

Granberry, J. (1993). The people who discovered Columbus: the prehistory of the Bahamas, a review and commentary. The Florida Anthropologist, 46(1), 56-60.

Huddleston, L. E. (2015). Origins of the American Indians: European Concepts, 1492-1729 (Vol. 11). University of Texas Press.

Keegan, William F. (1994). "West Indian archaeology. 1. Overview and foragers." Journal of Archaeological Research 2: 255–284.

Keegan, W. F., & Hofman, C. L. (2016). The Caribbean before Columbus. Oxford University Press.

MacNeish, R.S. (1964). Ancient Mesoamerican civilization. Science, 143: 531-537.

Needham, J (2004). Science and Civilisation in China. Volume 7, The Social Background. Part 2, General Conclusions and Reflections. Edited by Kenneth Girdwood Robinson, with contributions by Ray Huang. Introduction by Mark Elvin. Cambridge: Cambridge University Press.

Quest of the Carib Canoe (England: Think Tank/ BBC Television, 1999; VHS), directed by Eugene Jarecki

Reid, B. A. (Ed.). (2018). The archaeology of Caribbean and Circum-Caribbean farmers (6000 BC-AD 1500). New York: Routledge.

Ridley, R. T. (1986). To be taken with a pinch of salt: the destruction of Carthage. Classical Philology, 81(2), 140-146.

Roth, J. (2017) Sugar and slaves: The Augsburg Welser as conquerors of America and colonial foundational myths, Atlantic Studies, 14:4, 436-456, DOI: 10.1080/14788810.2017.1365279

Rouse, I. (1987). Whom did Columbus discover in the West Indies, American Archaeology, 6, 83-87

Rouse, I. (1991). Ancestries of the Taino: Amazonian or Circum-Caribbean. In Proceedings of the 13 International Congress for Caribbean Archaeology, edited by Edwin N. Ayubi and Jay B. Haviser. Reports of the Archaeological-Anthropological Institute of the Netherlands Antilles, (8), 682-702.

Rouse, I., (1992) The Tainos: Rise and Decline of the People Who Greeted Columbus, New Haven & London: Yale University Press

Russo, L. (2013). L'America dimenticata. Milan: Mondadori Università.

Sanoja, M. (1965). Venezuelan Archaeology Looking Toward the West Indies. American Antiquity, 31(2Part1), 232-236.

Socorro, O.A.A. 2006. Tesoros paleontológicos de Venezuela, el Cuaternario del Estado Falcón. Taima-Taima, Instituto del Patrimonio Cultural, p.120

Spiller, G. A. (2012). The Mediterranean diets in health and disease. Springer.

Thompson, G. (2010). Ancient Egyptian Maize I. Lulu.com Publishers.

Whitehead, N.L., 1984. Carib cannibalism. The historical evidence. Journal de la Société des Américanistes, pp.69-87

Writers of Eminence (1880). The National Encyclopaedia: A Dictionary of Universal Knowledge. London: William Mackenzie.

Chapter Three
Our Phoenician Alphabet

"The way is long if one follows precepts,
but short and helpful, if one follows patterns..."

Lucius Annaeus Seneca, Moral Letters to Lucilius,
Letter VI: On Precepts and Exemplars, Line 5

Moral Fables

The author hopes that the previous chapter has made clear that there were a host of distinct and defined native settlements and advanced civilizations settled in the Caribbean and South America, some who greeted Columbus when he arrived in 1492. It is in this context, following the Treaty of Tordesillas (1494) where a Spanish Pope Alexander VI divided the world in two between Spain and Portugal and gave Spain the larger share of the 'New World', that we can begin to discuss the Spanish province of Terra Firma (a territory comprised of modern-day Colombia, French Guyana, Guyana, Suriname and Venezuela) as the of 'Land of Do-as-you-please' and 'Take-what-you-want'.

The 'Land of Do-as-you-please' and 'Take-what-you-want' are children's stories that form part of the *Faraway Tree* (1943) series written by Enid Blyton during the Second World war, where the protagonists of the story visit places where they can literally do whatever they feel like doing and take whatever they feel like taking. No ifs or buts. Young readers are expected to appreciate how the allure of such a construct as unfettered horseplay is met by the trade-off of the chaos that may ensue from actions that occur in places devoid of sensible rules and ethical behaviour. Indeed, these moral fables continue to play a big part in the formation of young children's ethical and moral education in developed countries and are included as part of the curriculum alongside Aesop's Fables and Alice in Wonderland.

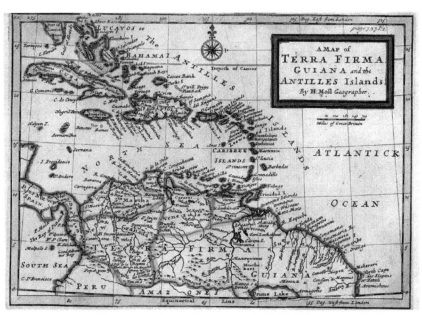

Figure 6: A Map Of Terra Firma by H. Moll from
Salmon, T. (1746), Modern History: or the Present State of All Nations Volume III

These moral fables where leadership is defined in terms of stewardship serve as an ideological antithesis to 'virtuous vanity', defined in this context as a sense of pride over being materialistic, selfish, arrogant and egotistic. In fact, leaders who act with a sense of duty and care to those who form part of their societies would invariably employ the common law construct of 'duty of care', a cornerstone of Tort in English Law. Indeed, what is Tort if not the act of codifying civil legal liability for the person who commits the tortious act, whether it is invasion of privacy, negligent infliction of physical or psychological injuries, financial loss or negligence. It is not for gains but rather for compensation that the remedy which lies at the heart of Tort, is to put the individual back to a position they would have been in but for the tortious act.

Nevertheless, because 'duty of care' is an overarching principle of English 'common law', when discussing the political leadership of Terra Firma, it would be more appropriate to do so within the legal framework of Equities and Trust. In Equities and Trusts the 'duty of care' is for the trustee to act in the best interest of the person with beneficial ownership. In the case of sovereignty, under Article 5 of the current Venezuelan constitution it states quite clearly that "non-transferable sovereignty resides in the people" (Venezuela, 1999). This means that beneficial ownership of Venezuela resides with its people, in simple terms, the Government and Legislature are legally bound to only act in the best interest of the people, rather than in accordance with their own interests.

However, it will come as no surprise to even the most casual observer of Venezuelan politics that this duty and the degree of transparency and honesty that it requires to function has not been fully understood by generations of Venezuelan politicians.

Moreover, when this political climate is coupled with the "feeling that the affairs of men are governed by forces that may be endured but not swerved from their movement" (Almond et al, 1989: 184), civic virtue, the foundation of all Democracies, comes under threat.

Chapter VIII articles 119-126 of Venezuela's constitution defines the rights of indigenous peoples within Venezuelan territory. Therefore, when a Venezuelan political leader fails to act in the best interests of the Venezuelan people and indigenous peoples of Venezuela, they are in breach of their 'duty of care'. What should follow is a legal challenge brought to Venezuela's Supreme Court, currently in exile, and yet in today's Venezuela, those legal challenges are impossible to enact and implement.

These checks and balances offered by legal remedies can serve to demonstrate the important role that moral fables concerning the importance of civic virtue, ethics, good governance and equity that are written for children and young adults can play in a society, especially in Venezuela, a country with a population distribution where proportionally there are more young people than adults. One might argue, statistically and morally, the role of educating those young people is paramount in order to develop competent citizens not just passive subjects.

However, the difficulty of such an endeavour has been primarily due to the fact that "Little Venice" (Roth, 2017: 439) or Venezuela, as it is now known, has developed a reputation over the last five hundred years of being a lawless place and adult playground for the most ruthless entrepreneurs and corrupt politicians; a real-life Westworld in Latin America, which perhaps inspired the popular sci-fi concept written and directed by Michael Crichton and released in 1973.

Take-what-you-want

Indeed, for over five hundred years, Venezuela has been ruled by individuals with a mandate to plunder its natural resources for *parias* (tribute) with little regard over social cohesion, by assuming social homogeneity, and a lack of desire to develop a degree of etiquette towards the distinct cultures that have come to define the different regions of Venezuela and their unique religious practices, for example, those of the Maria Lionza congregations of Chivacoa in Yaracuy State, which we will touch upon later in later books.

This list of statesmen includes the General Jose Antonio Páez (13 June 1790 – 6 May 1873), a low-ranking cowboy and cattle rustler who rose to become the first President of the independent Venezuelan Republic, and for his services to the Republic was awarded unceded lands inhabited by the Yaruro tribe in the Guachara Savanna region in modern day Apure State (Mitrani, 1988: 184), a man whose 'achievements' and the "revolutionary political culture" (Almond et al, 1989: 185) he represented we will cover in a later book.

Moreover, the land at the mouth of the Orinoco named *Tierra de Gracia* (Land of Grace) by Christopher Columbus in 1498, has since come to be known by the crude name *la Peninsula de Paria* (Peninsula of Tribute) in the years following Columbus' discovery. The relevance of *parias* (tributes) to our current notions of Venezuela and its people will be explored in more detail later on in this book.

When 'Take-what-you-want' and 'Do-as-you-please' has been practiced by Venezuela's statesmen for centuries it becomes a difficult task to imbue the idea that acts of plunder of this nature are both ethically and morally wrong to the general population. Also, when the non-native element of the general population arrives in Venezuela as part of expeditions that seek to turn conquest into profit, or as the slave labour intended to produce that profit, then profit can be said to be part of the equation from the start.

This commercialisation of people and lands, once normalised, may result in the current state of political and intellectual stasis, not to mention, social chaos that emerges from traditional values that are rooted in an antiquated colonial political structure founded and codified by Holy Roman Emperor Charles the V and further refined by the enlightened absolutism of King of Spain Charles III in 1777.

Nevertheless, in amongst the acts of human and mineral exploitation we find that in 1962 the Canaima National Park was established deep in the Amazon Rainforest with the aim of protecting the natural beauty and indigenous settlements established in the area. This National Park was designated a

UNESCO site in 1994. Moreover, as mentioned in the earlier chapter Taima-Taima was also made an Archaeological and Paleontological National Park following its discovery in 1962. We find also that the Natural Wonder that are the sand dunes of the 'Médanos de Coro' (Dunes of Coro) at the isthmus between the Venezuelan mainland and the Paraguana Peninsula, a short distance away from Taima-Taima was also designated a National Park in 1974. Indeed, the plethora of Venezuelan National Parks and volume of land designated as protected is truly astounding as shown below.

To understand the motivation for conservationism and the establishment of National Parks in Venezuela, that began in the 1930s with the establishment of 'Rancho Grande' (Large Ranch) as a National Park, later renamed Henri Pittier National Park after a distinguished Swiss scientist who classified over 30,000 plants in the country, we must first appreciate the change in mindset necessary to go from a resource driven mercantilism and exploitative practices to the patient and careful conservationist practices necessary to avoid resource depletion and the catastrophe described by Economist Thomas Malthus in 1798 as "famine...the last, the most dreadful resource of nature" (Malthus, 1798: 61).

Conservationist policies become the antithesis to exploitative practices. However, that is not to say anti-capitalist (since the Soviet Union was quite emphatically resource driven) but rather the type of 'Stakeholder Capitalism' described by Engineer and Economist Klaus Schwab, to appreciate that the overwhelming effect of the negative externalities on a population by a purely exploitative economic transaction will likely outweigh any profit gained.

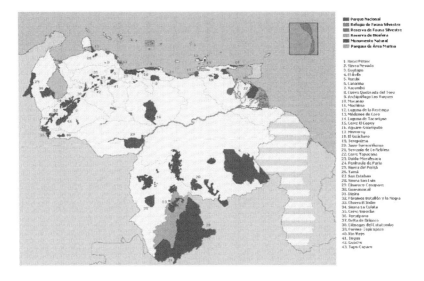

Figure 7: Venezuelan National Parks, Instituto Nacional de Parques

Nevertheless, despite the head start this established conservationism had in Venezuela by the late 1990s, since the dawn of 'Chavismo' these exploitative practices have returned with a vengeance and are currently threatening the flora and fauna found in these National Parks and the conservation efforts in these areas of outstanding natural beauty. Short-sighted and ruthless policies enacted with no regard for what game theorist Robert Axelrod called the "shadow of the future" (Axelrod, 1984: 124).

The Iberians

Historian Cecil Jane attempted to define the root cause of these short-sighted exploitative practices and the economic and intellectual stasis in Latin America by stating that it emerges from an undeniably *Castilian* nature. Meaning that it is a siloed outlook or mindset that has its origins in "the land of castles" (Jane, 1966: 21) of northern Spain, in stark contrast and perhaps challenging the poet John Donne's famous aphorism from his poem Meditation XVII that "no man is an island" (Donne, 1990: 58).

However, the reality is that the cultures that have shaped the peoples of the Iberian Peninsula are much older than the Visigothic Spain that Cecil Jane is alluding to. Indeed, before the dawn of Castile, recent DNA analysis of Neolithic human remains from various archaeological sites on the Iberian Peninsula have found "Anatolian Neolithic-associated ancestry in multiple regions of Iberia" (Olalde et al. 2019: 1231).

This DNA evidence coupled with the Upper Palaeolithic cave paintings found at the Cave of Altamira in Northern Spain dated at circa 35,000 BCE demonstrates how at the same time as the ancestors of the native Americans were making their way across the Bering strait, Neolithic Iberians were sheltering in caves and depicting their hunter gatherer lifestyle. Moreover, these early settlers of the territory that comprises modern day Spain are thought to have been Proto-Indo-Europeans who had migrated from Anatolia now modern-day Turkey, into Europe.

This view would support archaeologist Colin Renfrew's 'Anatolian Hypothesis' expressed in his book 'Archaeology and Language: The Puzzle of Indo-European Origins' (1987), a view which opposes the Kurgan Hypothesis that suggests the that the first settlers in Europe originated from an Indo-European migration from the Eurasian Steppe (Beckwith 2009: 32). Indeed, there is no reason to discount that the differing hypotheses are both true, since two separate migrations would not be out of the question.

Figure 8: Altamira Caves, Northern Spain ca.35,000 BCE

The wall paintings on the Neolithic Cave of Altamira serves to demonstrate how Iberia has been a place of suitable hunting grounds for hunter gatherers since at least 35,000 BCE Therefore, it is no surprise that the Andalusian red ochre ceramics found at *La Almagra* "covered with an iron oxide slip" (Chapman, 1990: 37) were initially deduced to have been made around 2000 BCE due to the existence of "similar pottery in the eastern Mediterranean"

(Chapman, 1990: 37). This hypothesis was later superseded by the ceramic findings at the Nerja cave, on the south coast of Andalusia which were made "at least 3,000 years before their alleged prototypes in the east Mediterranean" (Chapman, 1990: 38), meaning that around 5,000 BCE there appears to have been a civilization that made the 'La Almagra' (red ochre) clay pottery in southern Spain's Andalucía region.

The facial reconstruction unveiled in 2019 of a female's skull in amongst the Neolithic human remains found in the "Gorham's Cave" (Rodríguez-Vidala et al, 2014: 13301) Complex at Europa Point Gibraltar in 1996, and currently being exhibited at Gibraltar's National Museum, provides us with a forensic interpretation of what the early settlers who inhabited the island of Gibraltar over seven millennia ago may have looked like. The human female named 'Calpeia' by the British archaeologists working at Europa Point may have been a part of the same Neolithic Andalusian settlements that during the sixth millennium BCE experienced the arrival of the first agriculturalists that have been associated with the 'La Almagra' (red ochre) pottery of the region.

Controversially, some academics continue to believe that the red ochre ceramics "suggests a near east provenance" (Capel et al., 2006: 1157), even though "radio carbon dates have helped to clarify this position and disprove an east Mediterranean origin" (Chapman, 1990: 38). This may be because data on the Y-Haplogroup EM78 provides us with further clues regarding the possible origins of Calpeia and her people as "strongly suggestive of a north-eastern rather than eastern African origin" (Cruciani et al, 2007:1305) and of "trans-Mediterranean migrations directly from Africa…observed almost exclusively in Mediterranean Europe, as opposed to central and eastern Europe" (Cruciani et al, 2007:1307) from about 8,000 years ago.

Figure 9: Forensic Reconstruction of Neolithic Calpeia
buried at Europa Point approx. 5,500 BCE, Gibraltar Museum

Nevertheless, despite the origin of Calpeia's people, there is no reason to discount the hypothesis that red ochre ceramics could have been a technology developed in Andalusia by the Neolithic peoples who settled in the region. Moreover, the Semitic features shown in the forensic interpretation of Calpeia's remains is in line with the Y-DNA findings that southern Spain, specifically the island of Gadir (Cadiz) and Huelva may have had their origins as the Neolithic settlements of the migrating agriculturalists from Northern Africa.

What became of these Neolithic Andalusians may be pieced together from archaeological discoveries from the Late Bronze Age such as *The Ugaritic texts* written in cuneiform on clay tablets uncovered in the 1920s from Ras Shamra, Syria and the Late Bronze Age ovoid jugs from Byblos, Lebanon which have since shed a light on the culture the Celtic tribes of Europe and northern Spain encountered and labelled as Iberians. This name which is derived from the Celtic word *Bier* (river), presumably because to the Celts they were, quite literally, the "Riverians" (Nadeau & Barlow, 2013: 9) who lived across the waters of the Ebro (Latin: Ibērus flūmen) river near the western foothills of the Pyrenees.

Moreover, it is via Greek traders operating from their colony at Massalia circa 600 BCE (now known as Marseille, France) that we arrive at the written sources that mention the Bronze Age Iberian Chief Arganthonios, the ruler of Tartessos (Tharsis). Indeed, the name Arganthonios is curious in that it is a composite word made up of 'argantom' "the Celtic word for silver" (Harrison, 1988: 54), and root of the modern French word 'argent' (money), and the Greek word 'onios' (for sale). Curious that he may have been named 'Arganthonios' as a shorthand for other Greek traders. Indeed, the Greek name Tartessos given to the Iberians may have itself been a Hellenized form of the river Tertis, "the ancient name of the river Guadalquivir" (Harrison, 1988: 54) in southern Spain.

Nevertheless, evidence of boatbuilding and maritime trade in the Mediterranean can be traced back even further than 600 BCE. Although an early example of African mapmaking preserved by the 'Muzeo Egizio' in Turin is "an Egyptian map dating from about 1150 BCE" (Bassett, 2008: 1270) that serves to illustrate on papyrus an area called the 'Wadi Hammamat' between the Red Sea port of Quseir and the ancient city of Thebes, the act of Egyptian boat building has been represented in Egyptian art since Predynastic times (Berger, 1992: 107–120) c. 6000-3150 BCE. Indeed, sailing ships on the Mediterranean region date to at least 3000 BCE when the Egyptians began to use a bipod mast to support a single square sail on a vessel that mainly relied on multiple paddlers (Fig. 10). Later the mast would be developed to be a single pole, and the paddles would be supplanted with sturdier oars for greater speed. Such sailing vessels would have been initially designed to navigate the Nile and the Mediterranean coast.

Figure 10: Watercraft on a Predynastic Naqada II period vessel ca. 3500–3300 BCE, Metropolitan Museum of Art (36.1.121)

However, there is evidence that boat building during the Predynastic period was not restricted geographically to Egypt and the neighbouring Mediterranean. In Norway, depicted in the plethora of petroglyphs found in the Alta Fjord, near the Arctic Circle, we find an ancient example of an artist's depiction of Neolithic fishing dating from circa 4200 BCE. Indeed, just as Jean Paul Sartre reasoned that "existence precedes essence" (Sartre, 2007: 3), it becomes clear that technology precedes a successful human migration. In fact, one could argue that the Biblical Flood story of Noah in Genesis is a story of survival against insurmountable odds, due in part because of a technological advantage. Without the Ark, it is unlikely that Noah would have survived the catastrophic events of the flood at all.

Figure 11: Petroglyph featuring Neolithic fishermen,
Alta, Hjemmeluft, Bergbukten3A, Norway, c.4200 BCE

About 5,000 years after Calpeia's people may have settled in southern Spain, the islands of Ibiza and Gadir (Cadiz) would become Phoenician Bronze Age settlements and trade outposts around 1100 BCE These settlements formed part of the "established trade networks across the Mediterranean, reaching beyond the Straits of Gibraltar" (Zalloua et al, 2018: 2). However, Calpeia's facial features demonstrate how perhaps the already established influence of Northern African people in Southern

Spain may have aided in the establishment of Tyre's Canaanite outposts in southern Spain, Ibiza and Gibraltar which possibly eased the rise of a defined and successful Phoenician Bronze Age civilization. Moreover, the fact that "kinship pervades animal social organisation" (Krupp, 2008: 49), means that it is entirely possible that kinship amongst human populations would aid in the development of trade routes and cooperation.

The Naval Powers of Hesiod's Heroic Age

We know from archaeological evidence found in southern Spain that the province of Huelva, Andalusia has been home to mining settlements at Tharsis (Tartessos) since about 1250 BCE (Padilla-Monge 2016: 96) without a "hiatus that would have interfered with the continuity of the population" (Toscano, 2014: 142), the hiatus suggested by the archaeological evidence unearthed in the east Mediterranean and explored in historian Eric Cline's book '1177 B.C.: The Year Civilization Collapsed' (2014). The Tartessians were a Bronze Age civilization that had settled in southern Spain founded *Gadir* (Cadiz) as a port-city "extended from the Straits of Gibraltar to the mouth of the Guadalquivir" (Fleming 1915: 20) and by approximately 1000 B.C. through their developed expertise in mining and metallurgy of the natural resources available to them "had produced a remarkable development, celebrated throughout the ancient world." (Checkland 1967: 36).

Indeed, its people had refined a trifecta of "cultivation of the plain, the exploitation of the minerals of the hills and a vigorous oversea commerce" (Checkland 1967: 36) and thus became a

68

civilization very much a core part of the emergent ancient world and active participant in it. In fact, to mark the importance of its role in the ancient world we find it mentioned in both Hesiod's 'Theogony' and Pseudo-Apollodorus' 'Bibliotheke' in an account of Heracles' tenth labour to obtain the cattle of the three-bodied giant Geryon from the island of Erytheia (Gadir) also curiously described as 'Hera's Island' by the Greek geographer Strabo who mentions that "close to the Pillars [of Hercules] there are two isles, one of which they call Hera's Island; moreover, there are some who call also these isles the Pillars [of Hercules]" (Strabo, 3.5.3.). Therefore, the evidence appears to suggest a strong relationship between the port-city of Gadir (Cadiz) and the legend of the demi-god Hercules.

Figure 12: Sketch of an Attic black-figure amphora
(Heracles fighting Geryon) 550 B.C., Louvre, Paris

The Mari archives of Zimri-Lim serves as evidence to suggest that by the Late Bronze Age (c.1765 BCE) the Minoan ruler of the city of Knossos, in modern day Crete had a "fleet of merchant ships" (Foster, 2017: 346) that made regular trips to the Canaanite city of Ugarit. Moreover, around this time the Phoenicians of the Levant are believed to have had a merchant fleet of their own. Indeed, Phoenicia itself is believed to have been "a series of ports, with a rather narrow hinterland" (Quinn, 2018: 19). These ships were powered by square sails and sometimes with oars to supplement their speed. These types of vessels used a steering oar as a rudder to control direction (Anderson, 2003: 46).

The Greeks, who refer to themselves as the "Danaans" (Homer, 1924: Il. 2.485) in Homer's 'Iliad', proudly passed down a detailed account of their fleet, before it was written down as Homer's 'Catalogue of Ships' (Homer, 1924: Il. 2.484-759) in the second volume of his Iliad. In the catalogue Homer lists twenty-nine contingents under 46 captains, accounting for a total of 1,186 ships. Homer's Iliad, believed to have been written around 762 BCE is a second-hand account of events that are believed to have taken place around 1250 BCE. Over half a century after the events at Troy, the Danaans are believed to be mentioned again as the defeated 'Denye(n)' at the Battle of Djahy circa 1178 BCE, aa major land battle between the forces of pharaoh Ramesses III and a conglomerate academics call 'the Sea Peoples' (Edgerton, 1936: 53). It is these Sea Peoples who are historically believed to be those responsible for the destruction of Ugarit in 1175 BCE (Finkelstein et al., 2002: 87) when many of the great Civilizations of the day collapsed.

70

Bibliography

Almond, G. A., & Verba, S. (1989). The Civic Culture: Political Attitudes and Democracy in Five Nations. London et al.: Sage Publications.

Anderson, R., & Anderson, R. C. (2003). A short history of the sailing ship. New York: Dover Publications.

Apollodorus. (1921). Apollodorus, The Library, with an English Translation by Sir James George Frazer, F.B.A., F.R.S. in 2 Volumes. Cambridge, MA, Harvard University Press; London: William Heinemann Ltd.

Arteaga, O., Kölling, A., Kölling, M., Roos, A. M., Schulz, H., & Schulz, H. D. (2001). El puerto de Gadir. Investigación geoarqueológica en el casco antiguo de Cádiz, Rev. Atlántica-Mediterránea Prehist. Arqueol. Soc, vol.4, pp.345-416

Arteaga Matute, O., & Roos, A. M. (2002). El puerto fenicio-púnico de Gadir: una nueva visión desde la geoarqueología urbana de Cádiz. SPAL, 11, 21-39.

Bassett T.J. (2008) Maps and Mapmaking in Africa. In: Selin H. (eds) Encyclopaedia of the History of Science, Technology, and Medicine in Non-Western Cultures. Springer, Dordrecht. https://doi.org/10.1007/978-1-4020-4425-0_8717

Beckwith, C. I. (2009). Empires of the silk road: A history of central Eurasia from the Bronze Age to the present. Princeton University Press.

Berger, M. (1992). Predynastic Animal-Headed Boats from Hierakonpolis and Southern Egypt. The Followers of Horus: Studies Dedicated to Michael Allen Hoffman. Ed. Renée Friedman, and Barbara Adams. Oxford: Oxbow Books, pp.69–76

Berger M. (2008) Military Technology in Ancient Egypt. In: Selin H. (eds) Encyclopaedia of the History of Science, Technology, and Medicine in Non-Western Cultures. Springer, Dordrecht. https://doi.org/10.1007/978-1-4020-4425-0_9421

Bietak, M. (1991). Egypt and Canaan during the Middle Bronze Age. Bulletin of the American Schools of Oriental Research, 281(1), 27-72.

Blyton, E., & Winslet, K. (1943). The magic faraway tree. Egmont.

Capel, J., Huertas, F., Pozzuoli, A., & Linares, J. (2006). Red ochre decorations in Spanish Neolithic ceramics: a mineralogical and technological study. Journal of Archaeological Science, 33(8), 1157-1166.

Carretero, M. I., Pozo, M., Gómez Toscano, F., Ruiz Muñoz, F., Abad de los Santos, M., González-Regalado Montero, M. L., ... & Silva, P. (2010). 'Primeras evidencias de contaminación histórica en el Parque Nacional de Doñana (SO de España)', Studia Geologica Salmanticensia, 46 (1): pp. 65-74

Chapman, R. (1990). Emerging complexity: The later prehistory of south-east Spain, Iberia and the west Mediterranean. Cambridge University Press.

Checkland, S. G. (1967). The Mines of Tharsis: Roman, French and British Enterprise in Spain (Vol. 10). London, Allen, pp.36-40

Cline, E. H. (2014). 1177 BC: the year civilization collapsed. Princeton University Press.

Cruciani, F., La Fratta, R., Trombetta, B., Santolamazza, P., Sellitto, D., Colomb, E. B., ... & Moral, P. (2007). Tracing past human male movements in northern/eastern Africa and western Eurasia: new clues from Y-chromosomal haplogroups E-M78 and J-M12. Molecular biology and evolution, 24(6), 1300-1311.

Donne, J. (1990). Selection from Divine Poems, Sermons, Devotions, and Prayers. Edited by John Booty.

Edgerton, W.F., & Wilson, J.A. (1936) Historical Records of Ramses III: The Texts in Medinet Habu Volumes I and II. Studies in Ancient Oriental Civilization Vol. 12. University of Chicago Press

Finkelstein, I., & Silberman, N.A. (2002) The Bible Unearthed. New York et al.: Simon & Shuster

Fleming, W. B. (1915). The History of Tyre (Vol. 10). New York: Columbia University Press.

Foster, K. P. (2017). Mari and the Minoans. Historisch Tijdschrift Groniek, (217) Midden-Oosten.

Haber, M., Doumet-Serhal, C., Scheib, C., Xue, Y., Danecek, P., Mezzavilla, M., ... & Matisoo-Smith, E. (2017). Continuity and admixture in the last five millennia of Levantine history from ancient Canaanite and present-day Lebanese genome sequences. The American Journal of Human Genetics, 101(2), 274-282.

Harrison, R. J. (1988). Spain at the Dawn of History: Iberians, Phoenicians, and Greeks. London: Thames and Hudson.

Hesiod. (1914). The Homeric Hymns and Homerica with an English Translation by Hugh G. Evelyn-White. Theogony. Cambridge, MA.: Harvard University Press; London: William Heinemann Ltd.

Homer. (1924) The Iliad with an English Translation by A.T. Murray, Ph.D. in two volumes. Cambridge, MA., Harvard University Press; London: William Heinemann, Ltd.

Jane, C. (1966). Liberty and Despotism in Spanish America. Pref. by Salvador de Madariaga. New York: Cooper Square Publishers.

Krupp, D. B., Debruine, L. M., & Barclay, P. (2008). A cue of kinship promotes cooperation for the public good. Evolution and Human Behavior, 29(1), 49-55.

Malthus, T. R. (1798). An essay on the principle of population as it affects the future improvement of society, with remarks on the speculations of Mr Godwin, M. Condorcet, and other writers. London: J. Johnson.

Mitrani, P. 1988. "Los Pumé (Yaruro)". In "Los Aborígenes de Venezuela, Vol. III, Etnología Contemporánea II", edited by Jacques Lizot pp. 147–213. Fundación La Salle de Ciencias Naturales. , Caracas: Monte Avila Editores.

Olalde, I., Mallick, S., Patterson, N., Rohland, N., Villalba-Mouco, V., Silva, M., ... & Soares, P. (2019). The genomic history of the Iberian Peninsula over the past 8000 years. Science, 363(6432), 1230-1234.

Padilla-Monge, A. (2016). Huelva y el inicio de la colonización fenicia de la Península Ibérica. Pyrenae, 47(1), 95-117.

Renfrew, C. (1987), Archaeology and language: the puzzle of Indo-European origins. London: Jonathan Cape.

Pessini, L., de Barchifontaine, C. P., & Stepke, F. L. (Eds.). (2009). Ibero-American Bioethics: History and Perspectives (Vol. 106). Dordrecht: Springer Science & Business Media B.V.

Rodríguez-Vidala, J., d'Erricob, F., Pachecod, F. G., Blascoe, R., Rosellf, J., Jenningsh, R. P., ... & Carriónj, J. S. (2014). A rock engraving made by Neanderthals in Gibraltar. PNAS, 111(37), 13301-13306.

Roth, J. (2017) Sugar and slaves: The Augsburg Welser as conquerors of America and colonial foundational myths, Atlantic Studies, 14:4, 436-456, DOI: 10.1080/14788810.2017.1365279

Sartre, J. P. (2007). Existentialism is a Humanism. Yale University Press.
Strabo (1923). Geography, Volume II: Books 3-5. Translated by Horace Leonard Jones. Loeb Classical Library 50. Cambridge, MA: Harvard University Press.

Toscano, F. G. (2014). El Bronce Final en Huelva. Una visión preliminar del poblamiento en su ruedo agrícola a partir del registro arqueológico de La Orden-Seminario/Late Bronze Age at Huelva. A preliminary view of settlement patterns in its chora throught the study of the archaeological record of the Orden Seminario site. Complutum, 25(1), 139-158.

Venezuela, Bolivarian Republic of (1999) Constitution of the Bolivarian Republic of Venezuela.

Waal, W. (2018). On the 'Phoenician Letters': The Case for an Early Transmission of the Greek Alphabet from an Archaeological, Epigraphic, and Linguistic Perspective. Aegean Studies, 1, 83-125.

Zalloua, P. A., Platt, D. E., El Sibai, M., Khalife, J., Makhoul, N., Haber, M., ... & Arroyo, E. (2008). Identifying genetic traces of historical expansions: Phoenician footprints in the Mediterranean. The American Journal of Human Genetics, 83(5), 633-642.

Zalloua, P., Collins, C. J., Gosling, A., Biagini, S. A., Costa, B., Kardailsky, O., ... & Matisoo-Smith, E. (2018). Ancient DNA of Phoenician remains indicates discontinuity in the settlement history of Ibiza. Scientific reports, 8(1), 1-15.

Chapter Four
The Fertile Crescent

*"And Noah awoke from his wine, and knew what his younger son
had done unto him. And he said, cursed [be] Canaan; a servant of
servants shall he be unto his brethren. And he said, blessed [be]
the LORD God of Shem; and Canaan shall be his servant. God shall
enlarge Japheth, and he shall dwell in the tents of Shem; and
Canaan shall be his servant".*

Genesis 9:24-27

The Canaanites

The Neolithic agriculturalists who may have founded Calpeia's
Iberian civilization could have perhaps originated from the
Canaanite settlements that had emerged from the city of Byblos
in Canaan (Punic: 𐤂𐤁𐤋), a city that is believed to have been
inhabited since 5000 BCE, at a time when the city of Byblos stood
between a nascent Egypt to the south-east and pre-dated the
Akkadian Empire to the East and North of Byblos, by over two
millennia. Historically, the City State of Byblos had been the
source of the luxury cedar wood imported to Ancient Egypt (Tubb,
1998: 38) and to this day cedar trees are still a part of the modern
Lebanese national identity, which is why a green cedar tree is at
the centre on the modern Lebanese flag. Cedar trees can still be
found growing in modern Lebanon, especially in the 'Shouf Cedar
Reserve' in the centre of Lebanon.

Indeed, south east of modern Lebanon, a plethora of archaeological evidence pertaining to the Neolithic peoples of the Levant has been found concentrated around the 'Azraq Oasis' at the centre of the 'Azraq Basin' in modern day Jordan, currently the site of the shrinking 'Azraq Wetland Reserve'. An interesting linguistic point to note is that the Arabic word azraq (Arabic: أزرق) is still used as the word to describe the colour blue in modern Arabic and is the root for an old-fashioned Spanish word to describe blue-eyes (Spanish: Zarco) and also perhaps the root of the Spanish word for a puddle of water (charco), not to mention the Spanish word to describe the colour blue (Spanish: Azul).

Historically, in Europe most of what we knew of the history of Canaan (Punic: 𐤊𐤍𐤏𐤍) and the Canaanites including their city-states came from the Old Testament Biblical sources like the Table of Nations in Genesis chapters 10-11 which describes how the world was repopulated after the events of Noah's Ark and the great flood. In the Tanakh, Canaan is described as being a child of Ham, who begat Sidon, currently the third largest city in modern day Lebanon, north of the site where the ancient settlement of 'Sur' (Punic: 𐤑𐤓), the city better known as 'Tyre', once stood. These children of Ham are described as afterwards having "spread abroad" (Genesis 10.18).

However, recent Y-DNA comparisons from population samples across the Mediterranean, Middle East and Indian sub-continent with Neolithic human remains uncovered in the Fertile Crescent region of the Middle East, have shown that a Y-haplogroup J2 and specifically J2a, which originated in the Middle East, migrated from the Middle East to settle in Anatolia, South Caucasus and Iran around 12,000 years ago. A period that marks the end of the Last Ice Age.

Figure 13: Sketch of the 'Flood Tablet' (B10673), currently on display at the Penn Museum's Middle East Galleries in Pennsylvania.

One theory is that they may have migrated away from an ancient city at Dilmun in modern Bahrain, the ruins of which are still to this day a visitor attraction open to the general public. However, unlike the biblical account of Genesis found in the Torah, the Sumerian story of the paradise of Dilmun in 'Edin' (Sumerian for 'plain' or 'steppe'), or a region better known as Eden, was originally a post-diluvian story. This 'Eridu Genesis', a name coined by the historian Thorkild Jacobsen to describe this account found on the Nippur 'Flood Tablet' (B10673) preserved at the Penn Museum in Pennsylvania, USA, provides a pre-Eden Genesis story of creation and of the Great Flood which pre-dates, by over 1,000 years, the 6th Century BCE Genesis story of Adam and Eve that was written in the Torah whilst the Jews were held captive in Babylonia after the fall of Jerusalem in 586 BCE.

Bronze-Age Boat Builders

This clay 'Flood Tablet' (B10673) written in Sumerian around 1600 BCE, which has its provenance from an 1896 expedition funded by the University of Pennsylvania to Nippur (now modern day Nuffar, Iraq), describes how the Mountain goddess Nintur also known as Ninḫursaĝ the "Lady of the Mountains" (Langdon, 1917: 247), who we are also told is also responsible for the creation of mankind, one day decides "to call mankind home from a nomadic, vagrant existence, to have them build cities and temples, and thus become sedentary and civilised" (Jacobsen, 1981: 514). Moreover, in the text 'Eridu' is mentioned as the first city of mankind and the tablet also mentions the settlement's allotted portion of "half-bushel baskets" (Jacobsen, 1981: 518) and its dredged water canals for the irrigation of crops.

According to a "triangular fragment" (Langdon, 1915: 5) of the 'Paradise Tablet' (B4561), Enki is understood to have been the God who raised the waters for nine months with the help of the Goddess Ninḫursaĝ to dissolve man "like tallow and fat" (Langdon, 1915: 6). However, Ninḫursaĝ had created a plan to save a chosen few. In this much older version of the story dating from circa 1600 BCE, the King she saves is called 'Tagtug' and she

81

summons him and his entourage to a riverbank on the Euphrates where they embark "in a boat" (Langdon, 1915: 7).

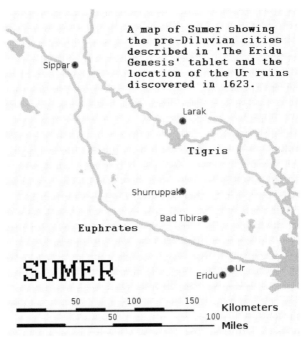

A map of Sumer showing the pre-Diluvian cities described in 'The Eridu Genesis' tablet and the location of the Ur ruins discovered in 1623.

Figure 14: A Map of Sumer c.4500:
The Settlements Mentioned in 'The Eridu Genesis' Tablet

However, in the 'Eridu Genesis' story, despite mankind's exceptionalism and longevity of life, the flood occurs because "Enlil took a dislike to mankind" (Jacobsen, 1981: 520). The reason for his dislike of mankind was that "....the clamour of their shouting...kept him sleepless" (Jacobsen, 1981: 520) and we can presume very cranky. So, he floods Sumer, leaving only Ziusudra who had the good fortune to have built a boat (Jacobsen, 1981: 524). Ziusudra or Zin-Suddu of Shuruppak the last king of Sumer prior to the Great Flood according to the Weld-Blundell Prism, displayed at University of Oxford's Ashmolean Museum.

The settlement at Eridu, on the Euphrates river near the most northern part of the Persian Gulf, is believed to be "the most famous centre of the cult of Enki the water god" (Langdon, 1915: 8), and is a short distance South-West from the city of Ur mentioned in the Bible as Abraham's hometown (Genesis 11: 31). Coincidentally, the ruins of the city of Ur had been buried under sand dunes when Italian Composer Pietro Della Valle stumbled across them in 1623 (Della Valle, 1892: 261) during his famous journey to India.

Moreover, it is interesting to note that like many of the indigenous civilizations encountered by the Spaniards in the New World, Professor Jacobsen states that in this early pre-diluvian civilization in Sumer it is believed that "all remuneration for work performed was accordingly given in goods, especially edibles such as grain or flour" (Jacobsen, 1981: 519). Therefore, the 'half-bushel baskets' would have served to define a particular settlement as an economic centre and place of barter exchange.

Hesiod's Golden Race Myth

These pre-diluvian peoples are described by the Greek poet Hesiod as the "Golden Race" (Jacobsen, 1981: 521) and they are described in 'The Eridu Genesis' tablet and by Hesiod as having had a childhood of 100 years. This understanding of ancient longevity and lengthy childhoods correlates with the biblical accounts in Genesis, for example, Methuselah was 187 years old when he begat his firstborn Lamech, and Lamech was himself 182 when he begat Noah (Genesis 5:28–31). However, according to the 'Paradise Tablet' this longevity of life comes to an end after the flood when 'Tagtug' arrives in "the land [of] Dilmun, the place where the sun rises" (Kramer, 1983: 121). Dilmun was known in ancient Sumer as the garden of the Gods and King 'Tagtug' was bestowed the role of gardener to their walled garden.

In the Bible, it is written that "the Lord God planted a garden in the east in Eden..." (Genesis 2:8). This garden in Eden or 'Edin', was quite literally a paradise. In fact, the origin of the word 'Paradise' or 'pardesu' in the Akkadian tongue meant a 'walled garden estate'. In late Hebrew 'pardes' came to mean an 'orchard or fruit garden' (Songs of Solomon, 4:13 and Ecclesiastes 2:5) and later on 'pardaysa' in Aramaic came to describe a 'royal park'. Indeed, to describe a place as paradise did not assume that it was a place as nature had intended, but rather that describing a place as a Paradise indicated a level of cultivation, gardening and biodiversity that only money could buy.

In some respects, that original meaning of paradise has remained with us and is made even more clear in the logical juxtaposition exploited for laughs in the old 'Gardener and the Vicar' joke which goes like this: A gardener had been hard at work tidying the Vicars' garden when the Vicar showed up to gaze upon his beautiful garden. He said to his gardener, "Sir, haven't God and you done wonders with this place?". There was a pause as the gardener rested from his work of trimming a rose bush and said "You should have seen this place when He had it all to Himself."

Unlike the Gardener in the joke, 'Tagtug' is bestowed with the title of God himself and is instructed that it is "forbidden...to eat of the cassia" (Langdon, 1915: 7). 'Tagtug' ignores these warnings and indulges in the fruit of the cassia, at which point "Ninḫursaĝ afflicted him with bodily weakness" (Langdon, 1915: 7). In modern times the cassia tree (*Cassia Fistula*) also known more commonly in botanical circles as 'golden shower' or 'purging cassia', is purely decorative. The tree bark itself and its seeds are toxic if ingested and the fruit is a known purgative or laxative. Ninḫursaĝ's warning would have been sound advice, as certainly ingesting the cassia fruit would have meant a very sudden and memorable trip to the lavatory for King 'Tagtug'.

In a way, the story of the fall of man in the Nippur 'Paradise Tablet' can be said to be the earliest example of toilet humour. Moreover, the Nippur 'Eridu Genesis' Tablet and the Nippur 'Paradise Tablet' both demonstrate a distinct relationship between mankind and their Gods. Whereas Noah's world is destroyed to eradicate sin and his Ark is rumoured to have ended up in the Mountains of northern Turkey, Ziusudra's civilization is destroyed by a sleep deprived God, because mankind failed to keep the noise down. In Tagtug's case, Enki destroyed mankind simply because he felt like it and wanted a change. Both stories are moral fables that would have been used to teach children about the importance of keeping quiet after nightfall and also in the case of the latter, an interesting way to teach children about the fickle nature of the wheel of fortune.

Figure 15: Sketch of the 'Paradise Tablet' (B4561), currently on display at the Penn Museum's Middle East Galleries in Pennsylvania.

Moreover, it must be noted that the Fall of Man story written in the 'Paradise Tablet' lacks the misogyny of the Adam and Eve story and describes instead the paradise of Dilmun as a walled garden, a gift from the Gods where the King was free to roam and tend the land. It is clear that the story may have been the inspiration for the Biblical story of Noah.

Ancient DNA

The oldest known J2a DNA samples were identified in remains from the Hotu Cave in northern Iran, dating from 9100-8600 BCE (Lazaridis et al., 2016), and from Kotias Klde in Georgia, dating from 7940-7600 BCE (Jones et al., 2015). This confirms that haplogroup J2 was already found around the Caucasus and the southern Caspian region during the Mesolithic period. The first appearance of J2 during the Neolithic came in the form of a 10,000-year-old J2b sample from Tepe Abdul Hosein in north-western Iran in what was then the Pre-Pottery Neolithic (Broushaki et al., 2016).

From these settlements the Y-haplogroup J2 has been found to have travelled westward as far as Hungary, 7,000 years ago (Sopot and Proto-Lengyel cultures in Hungary) and then during the Bronze Age westwards again via the Mediterranean into Crete, Cyprus, Sardinia, Spain and Northern Africa. It is believed that the J2a subclade may have been a dominant paternal lineage of the Early Bronze Age Kura-Araxes culture circa 3,400-2,000 BCE. Indeed, 32% of the modern-day male population of Crete has a direct lineage to the Y-haplogroup subclade J2a.

It may have given rise to a later culture which created the Khirbet Kerak-ware artefacts dated after the collapse of the Akkadian Empire circa 2154 BCE and found in both modern-day Syria and Canaan at the western edge of the Azraq basin, settled by the Neolithic peoples of the Levant where an Oasis was the central feature of an "extensive trans-boundary, renewable groundwater basin" (Janssens et al., 2013: 317). Populating a region with a vast underground aquifer would have been advantageous for the Neolithic peoples of the Levant, a water reserve which in its present state has sadly been exhausted of water, leading to the slow ecological collapse of the 'Azraq Wetland Reserve'.

A cubic regression analysis was carried out using annual precipitation data as the independent variable "to predict the frequency of Y haplogroups J1-M267, J2aM410 and J2b-M12" (Chiaroni et al., 2008: 285). The results for haplogroups J1 and J2a "correlated significantly with annual precipitation" (Chiaroni et al., 2008: 285). Therefore, the data may serve to demonstrate the importance of steady rainfall and a source of water to the spread of Y-haplogroup J2 6,000 years ago.

The J2a Y-haplogroup is believed to have spread into the northern region of the Fertile Crescent (Anatolia) during the Neolithic Period (King et al., 2011: 74) and into western Europe from around 1200 BCE (King et al., 2011: 69). Roy King notes a strong correlation between precipitation levels and associated levels of J2a population diffusion "consistent [with] a model of the cultural diffusion of agriculture" (King et al., 2011: 74).

Moreover, the "genetic memory retained in the extant distributions of Y-chromosome haplogroups J1-M267 and J2a-M410 within the Fertile Crescent significantly correlates with regional levels of annual precipitation" (Chiaroni et al., 2008: 285). This means that there is evidence of "statistically significant correlations [between] Y-chromosome haplogroups, precipitation levels and domestic lifestyle" (Chiaroni et al., 2008: 285). The "spatial frequency distribution of haplogroup J2a coincides closely with regions characterised by >400mm of annual precipitation capable of supporting settled agriculture, while haplogroup J1-M267 distributions correlate inversely with semi-arid regions characteristically used by pastoralists" (Chiaroni et al., 2008: 285).

Thus, these genetic researchers have been able to establish that the divergence in early population migration patterns between the J1 and J2 lineages seem to have been determined by their lifestyle and the importance of rainfall to an agricultural as opposed to pastoral community. It would then make sense that viticulture would likely mirror this spread since about 400 mm is also the level of annual precipitation required to support the farming of wine grapes (Winkler, 1974: 395). And this is what we see; that viticulture mirrors the proposed spread of M172, M410 through the Near east during the bronze age.

The Greek historian Thucydides, best known for his work the 'Peloponnesian War', wrote around the 5th century BCE, that "the people of the Mediterranean began to emerge from barbarism when they learnt to cultivate the olive and the vine" (Banilas, 2009: 402). Even in our own society we continue to associate culture and sophistication with the consumption of wine and olives. Indeed, the suggestion that Viticulture, the act of wine making, can be used to define the level of sophistication of an ancient culture is something that we accept without perhaps knowing the origin of this curious linguistic assumption at the root of the work 'culture'.

In the English language, we use the word 'culture' without perhaps understanding its roots as coming from the Latin word 'colere' (to till or to cultivate). In Latin a 'colonus' was a farmer and a 'colonia' was a farmstead. However, even to the ears of modern Spanish speakers, a 'colonia' is understood to be a colony rather than a farmstead, indicating the modern European shift away from the original meaning of the concrete noun to an abstract description of a group of people and their specific relationship to the territory they inhabit. Therefore, to colonize, should indicate a desire to cultivate and grow, but the long human history of subjugation and enforced tributary systems by colonists have somewhat redefined our modern usage of the word with negative undertones as a politically authoritarian and resource exploitative system.

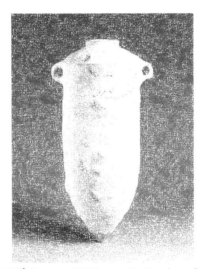

Figure 16: 6-5th Century BCE Terracotta Amphora (74.51.2300)
with Phoenician Inscription. Origin Cyprus. Currently at the Met Fifth Avenue, NY

Nevertheless, the male Y-Haplotype J2a group appear to have been 'colonists' in the original sense of the word. In fact, much like the Huguenots of the early-modern period, the Canaanites whether from Sidon, Byblos or Tyre appear to have been skilled tradesmen, selling their expertise, craftmanship skills, raw materials and wares at global markets for a profit. This is corroborated in Homer's 'Iliad' who describes the trophy at the Funeral Games in Honour of Patroclus, an ornate silver bowl the "Sidonians, well skilled in deft handiwork, had wrought it cunningly, and men of the Phoenicians brought it over the murky deep, and landed it in harbour" (Homer, Il. 23: 740). He also mentions that the embroidered robes of Priam's wife, Hecabe, were "the work of Sidonian women" (Homer, Il. 6: 285).

The Canaanite City-States of Ugarit, Sidon and Tyre

In the Bronze Age Canaan (Punic: יסנ) would become a buffer zone between Egypt to the south, Babylon to the East and Assyrians to the North. Indeed, the ebb and flow of trade and culture would be defined by vassalage and trade with their neighbours the great powers of the time. Nevertheless, we discover upon reading a specific Ugaritic text *The Ba'al Cycle* from tablets KTU/CAT 1.3 and 1.4 written by the Canaanites of the city-state of Ugarit around the 13th to 12th centuries BCE, that the main God of their Pantheon *El* (Deity) had 70 sons. The number of El's sons found in the Ugaritic texts coincide with the Jewish tradition that there were 70 first nations after Noah's flood, and is explained in the book of Deuteronomy as the boundaries set "according to the number of the sons of God" (Deuteronomy 32.8).

Following the collapse of civilizations around 1177 BCE and the decline of Egyptian influence in the Levant from around 1200 BCE, the city-states of Canaan "were freed from foreign domination"

91

(Department of Ancient Near Eastern Art, 2004). This meant that the Canaanites had the freedom to expand, grow and seek new markets abroad. Moreover, not only did the Canaanites seek to populate regions where the act of cultivation would be easier, but also, they demonstrate that their drive for cultivation was equalled by their ability to set up successful settlements outside of their immediate sphere of influence. It is interesting to note that not only has the J2a Haplotype been found in mainland Spain, but that it has also been found to have travelled eastwards into the Indian subcontinent, specifically the regions of Punjab, Gujarat and Rajasthan in modern day India and the Sindh region in modern day Pakistan known as the location of the Bronze Age Indus Valley Civilization with its largest city at Mohenjo-Daro.

A curious fact, is that the breakthrough in translating the cuneiform tablets from Ugarit was largely due to the good fortune that the team of French archaeologists led by Charles Virolleaud noticed the relationship between the Ugaritic/Punic abecedary and the modern Hebrew abecedary which then allowed them to begin to attempt to translate the clay tablets in the 1930s. Charles Virolleaud subsequently wrote the two first seminal texts on the Phoenicians based on his findings: 'La Civilisation phénicienne' (1933) and 'La Mythologie phénicienne' (1937).

An understanding of the Canaanite pantheon can help us understand the Biblical symbolism of the Old Testament, the 'Labours of Hercules' and the emergence of the 'Holy Trinity' at the core of Roman Catholic belief which spread throughout Europe. Although the two cultures of Tyre and Israel had already begun to drift apart by the time a fixed version of the Tanakh came to be written around 140 BCE there is a lot that the Tanakh can tell us about its proto-sinaitic roots if we read between the lines.

Figure 17: Sketch of RS 12.063-KTU 5.6 c.1200 BCE
The transcription of the alphabetic sign list is: (1) ʾa b g ḫ d h w z ḥ ṭ y k š l;
(2) m d n ẓ s ʿp ṣ q r t; (3) ġ t ʾ ủ ṩ

ʾalp	bêt	gaml	digg	hô	wô (waw)	zê(n)	ḥê(t)	yad	kapp
lamd	mêm		naḥš (šamk?)		ʿên	piʾt	ṣa(d)	qu(p)	
raʾš	ṭann	tô (taw)							

Figure 18: Proto-sinaitic Abjad circa. 1850 BCE

The Book of Daniel in the Ketuvim

This understanding of the Canaanite pantheon also lends itself to a hypothesis that the Angel Michael described in the 6th century BCE context of the book of Daniel (Daniel 10:13-21) is a derivation of "El's supreme son...Baal, the chief and most active of the gods under El" (Day, 2020: 175). The significance of the Angel Michael remaining unchallenged in the Jewish liturgy in spite of rabbinical prohibition against appealing to intermediaries is not something that should be overlooked and may suggest the continued importance of Ba'al worship.

Therefore, we can conclude that Ba'al (Lord) may have been one of Canaan's more active, heroic and warlike guardian angels, which is why the Book of Daniel makes mention of him, especially during a time of captivity. While the Ugaritic text 'The Ba'al Cycle' depicts him as challenging and outwitting Mot, a personification of Death to bring back the earth from the brink of chaos, a similar story to that of the Canaanite Lion headed God of War 'Mekal' is found in Egypt, of a Lion headed God known as 'Maahes' to the Egyptians, who defended Ra's solar barque on a daily basis against attacks from the serpent Apophis or Apep, an enemy of Ra's, during the sun's night time's visit through the underworld.

Moreover, quite importantly Lion headed 'Maahes' associated with war and protection was also believed to devour captives, which may explain the significance of the visions of the Angel Michael in the Book of Daniel and the Lions who leave the captive Daniel from Judah unharmed. It is curious that Mekal or Maahes, which may have been known as Melqart in the northern Canaanite city-state of Tyre (Punic: 𐤌𐤋𐤒𐤓𐤕), the capital city of the Phoenician Empire, would also symbolise the annual cycle of vegetation. Furthermore, it is fascinating to note the use of Lions in the Book of Daniel as symbols of divine judgement, and how the Lion to this day remains a symbol associated with the people Judah, the state of Israel and a symbol used to describe Jesus Christ. Indeed, just as Melqart also came to be associated with the city-state of Tyre and gained messianic status as Hercules.

The link between the hero Hercules/Herakles who is known for wearing the skin of a Lion in battle and the Phoenician deity Melqart is described by the Roman Geographer Pomponius Mela who confirms this as a fact when he describes Melqart's Temple at Gades (Cadiz) as founded by the Phoenicians and the place where "Hercules' bones are buried" (Pomponius Mela III 41). It appears therefore, that the Lion at the core of Iberian sensibilities and the pillars that to this day adorn either side of Spain's coat of arms have their origin in Ba'al's followers, the children of Canaan.

Bibliography

Arteaga, O., Kölling, A., Kölling, M., Roos, A. M., Schulz, H., & Schulz, H. D. (2001). El puerto de Gadir. Investigación geoarqueológica en el casco antiguo de Cádiz, Rev. Atlántica-Mediterránea Prehist. Arqueol. Soc, vol.4, pp.345-416

Arteaga Matute, O., & Roos, A. M. (2002). El puerto fenicio-púnico de Gadir: una nueva visión desde la geoarqueología urbana de Cádiz. SPAL, 11, 21-39.

Banilas, G., Korkas, E., Kaldis, P., & Hatzopoulos, P. (2009). Olive and grapevine biodiversity in Greece and Cyprus—a review. In

Climate change, intercropping, pest control and beneficial microorganisms (pp. 401-428). Springer, Dordrecht.

Bietak, M. (1991). Egypt and Canaan during the Middle Bronze Age. Bulletin of the American Schools of Oriental Research, 281(1), 27-72.

Broushaki F, et al. (29 July 2016). Early Neolithic genomes from the eastern Fertile Crescent. Science. 353(6298):499-503.

Burkert, W. (1985). Greek religion. Cambridge, MA.: Harvard University Press.

Carretero, M. I., Pozo, M., Gómez Toscano, F., Ruiz Muñoz, F., Abad de los Santos, M., González-Regalado Montero, M. L., ... & Silva, P. (2010). 'Primeras evidencias de contaminación histórica en el Parque Nacional de Doñana (SO de España)', Studia Geologica Salmanticensia, 46 (1): pp. 65-74

Chiaroni, J., King, R. J., & Underhill, P. A. (2008). Correlation of annual precipitation with human Y-chromosome diversity and the emergence of Neolithic agricultural and pastoral economies in the Fertile Crescent. Antiquity, 82(316), pp.281-289.

Department of Ancient Near Eastern Art (October 2004). "The Phoenicians (1500–300 B.C.)." In 'Heilbrunn Timeline of Art History'. New York: The Metropolitan Museum of Art, 2000–. http://www.metmuseum.org/toah/hd/phoe/hd_phoe.htm

Haber, M., Doumet-Serhal, C., Scheib, C., Xue, Y., Danecek, P., Mezzavilla, M., ... & Matisoo-Smith, E. (2017). Continuity and admixture in the last five millennia of Levantine history from ancient Canaanite and present-day Lebanese genome sequences. The American Journal of Human Genetics, 101(2), 274-282.

Hesiod. (1914). The Homeric Hymns and Homerica with an English Translation by Hugh G. Evelyn-White. Theogony. Cambridge, MA.: Harvard University Press; London, William Heinemann Ltd.

Homer. (1924) The Iliad with an English Translation by A.T. Murray, Ph.D. in two volumes. Cambridge, MA., Harvard University Press; London, William Heinemann, Ltd.

Jacobsen, T. (1981). The Eridu Genesis. Journal of Biblical Literature, 100(4), 513-529. doi:10.2307/3266116

Janssens, S., & Thill, Z. (2013). Water in Azraq (Jordan): a fluid link between state and society. Journal des anthropologues. Association française des anthropologues, (132-133), 317-338.

Jones, E., Gonzalez-Fortes, G., Connell, S. et al. (2015). Upper Palaeolithic genomes reveal deep roots of modern Eurasians. Nat Commun 6, 8912.

Kenneson, P. D. (1999). Life on the Vine: Cultivating the Fruit of the Spirit. InterVarsity Press.

King, R.; Dicristofaro, J.; Kouvatsi, A.; Triantaphyllidis, C.; Scheidel, W. et al. (2011) The coming of the Greeks to Provence and Corsica: Y-chromosome models of archaic Greek colonization of the western Mediterranean. BMC Evolutionary Biology, BioMed Central, 11 (1), pp.69-76.

Kramer, S. (1983). The Sumerian Deluge Myth: Reviewed and Revised. Anatolian Studies, 33, 115-121. doi:10.2307/3642699

Langdon, S. (1915) Sumerian Epic of Paradise, the Flood and the Fall of Man, (Vol. 10, No. 1). University Museum, pp. 5-8.

Langdon, S. (1917). The Necessary Revisions of the Sumerian Epic of Paradise. The American Journal of Semitic Languages and Literatures, 33(3), 245-249.

Lazaridis, I., Nadel, D., Rollefson, G. et al. (2016). Genomic insights into the origin of farming in the ancient Near East. Nature 536, 419–424.

Pessini, L., de Barchifontaine, C. P., & Stepke, F. L. (Eds.). (2009). Ibero-American Bioethics: History and Perspectives (Vol. 106). Springer Science & Business Media.

Toscano, F. G. (2014). El Bronce Final en Huelva. Una visión preliminar del poblamiento en su ruedo agrícola a partir del registro arqueológico de La Orden-Seminario/Late Bronze Age at Huelva. A preliminary view of settlement patterns in its chora throught the study of the archaeological record of the Orden Seminario site. Complutum, 25(1), 139-158.

Virolleaud, C. (1933). La civilisation phénicienne d'après les fouilles de Ras-Shamra. Annales de l'Université de Paris, pp.397-415.

Virolleaud, C. (1937). La mythologie phénicienne d'après les poèmes de Ras-Shamra. Annuaires de l'École pratique des hautes études, 50(47), 5-19.

Wasilewska, E. (2000). Creation stories of the Middle East. Jessica Kingsley Publishers.

Winkler, A. J., Cook, J.A., Kliewer, W. M., & Lider, L. A. (1974) General Viticulture. Second Edition, Edited by Laura Cerruti. California: University of California Press.

Yon, M. (1997). La cité d'Ougarit sur le tell de Ras Shamra. Paris: Ed. Recherche sur les civilisations.

Chapter Five

A Story Written in Egypt

*"It was a beam that broke...then the boat sank,
and of those aboard none remained".*

**The Story of the Shipwrecked Sailor: Lines 37-39
Written circa 2000 BCE.**

The Tree of Life

Nothing is born from nothing. We ourselves are only one part of the story of the complete journey of our genetic material, that through chance or, in some cases, some planning, have arrived at our current pit-stop in an unforeseen future destination. The emerging promise of a foetus in a womb is much the same as the emerging promise evident in a nascent people. In previous chapters, we have discussed the long journey of the indigenous tribes of Latin America, the centres of civilization in Mesopotamia and the culture of the Canaanites in the Levant. However, it is clear that we are yet to discuss the elephant in the room, the goliath of the ancient world, the Kingdom of Egypt.

In this chapter, we will begin by discussing Egypt in the context of the Old Kingdom text 'The Story of Sinuhe' dated from circa 1900 BCE (Assmann, 2005: 177) to find out what the text can teach us about the Semitic communities of the Levant at the time it was written. It must be noted that the name Sinuhe was a composite

100

of two words, 'Sa' (Sa:🦆) and 'Nht', followed by a tree (🌳) terminative. In Ancient Egyptian, 'Sa' meant 'son of '(Sa:🦆), represented by a hieroglyph of a 'duck', and the noun 'Nht' meant Sycamore (Hoffmeier, 2005: 256) when followed by a tree terminative (🌳). The name of the protagonist Sinuhe demonstrates the significance of the sycamore tree to his story, especially when we come to understand that the Sycamore tree (Ficus sycomorus) represented the Egyptian 'tree of life'. The noun 'Nht' may have also had the meaning of 'refuge' when written with a "house terminative (⌂) instead of the tree" (Buhl, 1947: 80).

The Biblical story of Joseph is believed to have been derived from this classical story from antiquity. At first glance, the story of a young man working as a royal official, who escapes Egypt and flees to Canaan following news of the assassination of his leader Amenemhat I, might not appear to draw parallels with the Biblical story of Joseph. However, at its core 'The Story of Sinuhe' demonstrates a challenge posed by the politics and ambitions of elites that fall outside of our protagonist's control. Nonetheless, despite the adversity posed by those challenging times, our protagonist overcomes those obstacles to rise to a position of power, and in the end, is rewarded by being reconciled with his homeland. It is clear in that context that the stories of Sinuhe and Joseph in Genesis "present reversed or mirror-image examples of the same motif" (Meltzer, 2004: 79), with Sinuhe fleeing to the Levant and later being reconciled with his beloved Egypt, while Joseph was sold as a slave to Egypt and was later reconciled with his family in the Levant.

Moreover, in the story of Sinuhe we can also find parallels between the Goddess Hathor as the 'Lady of the Sycamore' (Keel, 1992: 86-87), alluded to in the text, and the Goddess Ninḫursaĝ the 'Lady of the Mountains' of Ancient Sumer. In both cases, these feminine Goddesses can be seen as fundamental extensions of the African Deity 'Mami Wata', a worship that can be seen throughout Africa and was even exported to the Americas via the slave trade (Drewal, 2008: 1). These Lady life-givers represent the same role as Ninḫursaĝ, the Flood Tablet's 'Lady of the Mountains' and creator of mankind. A worship of water as the giver of life, embodied by its source, whether a tree or mountain or a fig, to become holy sites that are represented in the form of the sacred feminine.

To some in our modern world, the significance of the sycamore fig tree (Ficus sycomorus) might not be especially noteworthy. Moreover, if you are reading this from a country in the northern hemisphere you might confuse the sycamore fig (Ficus sycomorus) with the sycamore maple (Acer pseudoplatanus). As anyone from Canada would attest, the reason for the Maple's importance in the anglosphere is that if you notice a host of sycamore trees (Acer pseudoplatanus) concentrated in a particular area, there is a high probability that you will find a source of water nearby. It is nature's clue for a plentiful source of water as sycamore trees require a lot of water to grow from seed to saplings. Moreover, as with another tree from the genus Acer, the Maple, the Sycamore can be tapped for its sugary syrup, a life saver in times of famine.

However, in contrast to the Sycamore maple, the Sycamore fig tree (Ficus sycomorus) is a species native to the tropical climates of the Middle East and Africa and can still found in modern day Cyprus, Egypt, Israel, Kenya, Lebanon, Nigeria South Africa, and the southern United States. In the northern part of Nigeria, the Sycamore fig is found to thrive in soils near streams in the savannah region (Adoum et al., 2012: 4095) with plenty of fig-wasps to pollinate the tree's flowers (Shanahan, 2016: 99) and bear fruit, while in Kenya, a distinct species of fig tree called 'Mugumo' (Ficus natalensis) has come over the millennia to represent a tree sacred to the Kikuyu people.

To the Ancient Egyptians at Memphis, a city at the mouth of the Nile delta, the Sycamore fig tree came to represent the Goddess Hathor, the mother of the Gods Ra and Horus who represented the Sun and the Sky respectively, as a "tree-goddess" (Buhl, 1947: 86). Hathor is also said to be the one who healed the eye of Horus with the milk from a gazelle. Therefore, the 'Lady of the sycamore' (Keel, 1992: 86-87) is evidently both a caregiver and a healer. In the family tomb of Sennedjem built circa 1250 BCE, now a tourist attraction in modern Deir el-Medina, Egypt, the Goddess Hathor is depicted as tree-goddess looking after Sennedjem and his wife Ly-neferti in the afterlife.

The Sycamore fig can be distinguished from other varieties of fig trees by its heart shaped leaves, pink fruit, white sap with anti-bacterial and antiseptic qualities, and a dry tree-bark that can serve as the ideal as a soft wood friction base to be used for fire-starting. It must be noted that the juice from the fig and the latex from its leaves are both milky white liquids and as such were known to the ancient Egyptians as 'milk' from the sycamore. Indeed, because of its antiseptic properties when applied topically, the latex from the sycamore fig can be used to heal cuts, abscesses, and wounds. It makes sense that the Tree of Life would heal and thus provide a longer life. A fruit that represented eternal love and the divine feminine. Indeed, even today in Europe figs still represent female sexuality. To the Israelites, it may be this reason why perhaps in later interpretations of the Eden story, the tree came to represent their Tree of Knowledge rather than the Tree of Life in the 'Fall of Man' story in Genesis.

Figure 19: Tomb of Thutmose III, depicting King Thutmose suckling from the Goddess Hathor who has taken the form of a Sycamore.

This shift may demonstrate that a certain level of humourlessness had taken over the religious Israelite narrative of Eden by the time Genesis was penned. Indeed, to teach a population that the 'Tree of Life' is a forbidden 'Tree of Knowledge' that led to the 'Fall of Man' at the hands of Eve, and at the same time discard the

Sumerian warning of the cassia tree, due to its humorous yet crude punchline, may show a cruel intention to sow ignorance and learned helplessness. Nevertheless, in modern-day Bahrain, believed to be the home of Eden, the myth of the 'Tree of Life' continues to endure as a symbol of fertility and bounty amidst a barren landscape in the physical embodiment of a 500-year-old Acacia tree. Water as a life giver serves to further contextualise the 'Flood Tablet' with a sense of irony that the resource that is associated as the giver of life is that which at the same time had the power to take it away.

Bloody Borders

Contrary to popular belief, the Israelites as a people or nation would not have been formed in a vacuum, but rather, like any other co-operative group emerged due to circumstance. The Israelites as a nation of people may have indeed been born as an antithesis to Egypt's Pharaohs but also as we discussed earlier as a group that sought to be distinct from the people of Canaan. Historian Israel Finkelstein discusses the story of Exodus in this context and reasons that "legends of liberation from Egypt could have been skilfully woven into the powerful saga" (Finkelstein et al., 2000: 68) of Exodus.

In Historian Peter Turchin's book 'War and Peace and War', we find a discussion of "metaethnic frontiers" (Turchin, 2007: 5) that seeks to describe territories that have historically been zones of conflict between distinct groups of human beings. Whether it is the Greeks versus the Trojans, Leonidas versus Xerxes, or the

Allies versus the Axis Powers, these frontiers have been at the forefront of human conflict and war. Nevertheless, it is clear that Turchin's blood-soaked frontiers are simply a re-wording of what Samuel P. Huntingdon called "bloody borders" (Huntington, 1993: 35), in this seminal paper 'Clash of Civilizations', in which he focused a lot of his attention on the Middle East.

Figure 20: Pargeting in U Sv. Ducha, Prague, Chechia
'VE SVETOVE VALCE' (In the World War)

As described in an earlier chapter, in the Late Bronze Age, Canaan (Punic: כנען) was a buffer zone between three warring tribes: Egypt to the south, Babylon to the East and the Assyrians to the north. Moreover, in the Early Bronze Age this had not changed, and Canaan can still be seen as a buffer zone between Egypt to the south and the Hittites to the north. As a buffer zone, much like Belgium was in the Napoleonic, First and Second world wars, Great Power Nations normally treat those territories as their battle arenas. In the case of Belgium, it is no coincidence that it is the home to Waterloo, Flanders and the first entry point of invasion for the German Blitzkrieg offensive, despite Belgium's stance of neutrality against Germany at the time.

Indeed, much like any river which carves its place out of the landscape, a well-trodden path normally presents the path of least resistance and most economic and political advantage for the individuals pursuing that path. In north Africa, arguable a Bronze Age 'metaethnic frontier' we can provide two examples of Semitic Kingdoms, which came to rival the Great Powers of their time, the Hyksos, and the Carthaginians. In both cases, they began with an Exodus driven by a need to seek alternate markets to make a living.

The first of the peoples we will discuss, the 'Hyksos' of the Nile delta, may serve to demonstrate where the technological distinction that turned the Canaanites tribes of the Levant into the literate Phoenicians of Tyre may have begun. Moreover, the second of these Semitic north African peoples, the 'Carthaginians', might help us to fill in the gaps over what may have become of the Phoenicians after the Assyrian King Nebuchadnezzar II laid siege to their Capital city Tyre or 'Sur' (Punic: 𐤑𐤓) in 586 BCE Tyre for 13 years. These two examples may show how politics, technology and geography can all serve to determine a cultural institution's influence over the morphological changes in the long-term development of a culture's symbols, laws, history and social structure.

In the Bible, a shorthand for the story of the 'Hyksos' is believed to be the text of Moses in Exodus. Historian Israel Finkelstein states that "immigration of Canaanites to Egypt and their expulsion from the delta in the second millennium BCE" (Finkelstein et al., 2000: 69) may have served as the inspiration for the liberation story of Exodus which is believed to have occurred during the reign of the Pharaoh Ramses II. However, as we will uncover, the real story of Exodus is much more nuanced than that told in the Bible as the escape of an enslaved people made possible by the miracle of the parting of the Red Sea. As millions of ordinary Venezuelans currently fleeing or having fled their homes in the recent two decades will tell you, an Exodus of people is a telling symptom of human suffering rather than its cause.

In contrast to the Pyramid Age, during the Egyptian Feudal Age circa 2000 BCE we find evidence that "reveals progress in a higher realm, that of conduct and character" (Breasted, 1916: 76). A plethora of stories and non-fiction texts written in papyrus like 'The Story of Sinuhe', "the beginnings of geometry and elementary algebra" (Breasted, 1916: 78), that demonstrate a rise in abstract and critical thinking fundamental to building a more connected world. Moreover, it is at this time that the Ancient Egyptians may have "dug a canal from the north end of the Red Sea westward to the nearest branch of the Nile in the eastern delta" (Breasted, 1916: 79) a proto-Suez Canal, that would have linked the Mediterranean with the Indian sub-continent. Indeed, the use of this canal would have meant that "the Pharaoh's Mediterranean ships could sail up the easternmost mouth of the Nile in the eastern Delta [and]...reach the Red Sea" with ease, opening up trade routes far beyond the shores of Egypt.

It is around this time of the second millennium BCE, that we also encounter three further curious pieces of evidence. The first, is 'The Story of the Shipwrecked Sailor' (Tappan, 1914: 41) written circa 2000 BCE. It is the story of a sailor who was travelling in open water on a ship with a crew of 150 men, "one hundred and fifty cubits [in] length" (Tappan, 1914: 43) and a "width of...forty cubits" (Tappan, 1914: 43), in modern units, it describes a vessel roughly 68 meters (223 ft) in length and 18 meters (59 ft) in width. By today's standards, that size vessel would be classed as a Superyacht, which in the story was destroyed by waves "eight cubits" (Tappan, 1914: 43) or 3 meters high.

It is clear from the story that navigating in open water in a large vessel circa 2000 BCE was not uncommon, especially to sail to the Pharoah's mines in the land of Punt, now a territory in modern-day Ethiopia and Somalia, to pick up raw minerals. To request help from the Gods the Egyptian protagonist offers a burnt offering to the gods as an act of faith. He describes a secondary character, the snake, as being adorned with gold and lapis-lazuli, a rare blue gem mined in Afghanistan, and the island he is stranded in as being full of sycamore figs and grapes.

Later in the story, the gifts offered to the protagonist by the snake are luxury items like incense, perfumes, cassia wood (still used as incense in modern Sudan), kohl (eyeliner) and cypress wood (very aromatic). Furthermore, in the story the protagonist describes bravery in terms of their "hearts of whom were stronger than lions" (Tappan, 1914: 43). Demonstrating the clear written association around 2000 BCE between a lion's ferocity and a man's ability to withstand adversity or demonstrate bravery, an association which will become an important distinction of the people of 'Avaris' in the eastern part of the Nile delta from around 1715 BCE to 1580 BCE.

The second, is the archaeological evidence on Pharaoh Userkare Khendjer from Abydos, the 21st Pharaoh of the XIII Dynasty around circa 1760 BCE. This Pharaoh is believed by some historians to have been a 'Hyksos' because his name "may be of Semitic origin" (Beckerath, 1958: 265) rather than Egyptian. However, within the context of an existing canal in the eastern Nile delta that connected the Nile with the Red Sea, as mentioned by Historian James Breasted, it may be plausible to presume that a Semitic merchant class may have emerged in that area and chosen to establish themselves and settle in northern Egypt, intermarried with Egyptians and even risen to become the rulers of Memphis at the mouth of the Nile over a period of hundreds of years.

The third, is an association between the first letter of the Phoenician abjad 'aleph' (Punic: 𐤀), its significance as a symbol denoting the "head of cattle" (Mailhammer et al., 2019: 147) and the previously mentioned Goddess Hathor, who is often depicted as a cow. The horns therefore may have come to represent our equivalent of a halo, a symbol of holiness found in representations of the Semitic Goddess Aštart (Punic: 𐤏𐤕𐤓𐤔𐤏), a fertility or love Goddess typically associated with Venus-Aphrodite, Hathor, the morning star (Venus) and cattle worship. It might be interesting to note that the first letter of runic alphabet 'fehu' (Norse: ᚠ), also meant cattle and came to mean wealth (Mailhammer et al., 2019: 149).

Therefore, it may stand to reason that 'faith' as a construct was a way, to paraphrase 'The Hunger Games Series' author Suzanne Collins, to make sure the odds remained in an individuals' favour. Moreover, we see good fortune as 'divine intervention' in the Roman dice game of 'Tali' where the luckiest throw of fourteen was referred to as a 'Venus throw' and due to Venus' 'green-flash' effect as it sets, the colour green may have also been culturally associated with good luck. It is quite fascinating to note that in over four thousand years, despite our technological advances, human nature has remained as it always has been, driven by luck, aspiration, fear, and ambition to achieve a better life. In games of chance, luck is integral for success.

With this in mind, archaeological evidence from the Middle Bronze Age dating from a period a few hundred years after the assassination of Amenemhat I circa 1962 BCE, described in 'The Story of Sinuhe', and before the cuneiform Ugaritic texts, mention the Semitic 'Hyksos', the name itself a 'Hellenized' form of the name given to them by the Egyptian Pharaohs, 'Heqa-Khaset'. This word was translated by historian Flavius Josephus as "King Shepherds" (Josèphe, 2000: 56), but was in fact, an amalgamation of the two hieroglyphs 'Heqa' (𓋾) an Egyptian 'Shepherd's Crook' a symbol of royalty, and 'Khaset' (𓈉) which was used as a determinative Hieroglyph for 'foreign land' or 'foreigner'. There was no political correctness in Ancient Egypt, so we find that when used together these hieroglyphs would have been used by an Egyptian stonemason to denote the leader of the Hyksos Abi-Shai circa 1890 BCE, as a "Chief of Foreign Lands" (Goedicke, 1984: 208).

If a canal did exist and it served to join the Mediterranean with the Red Sea, the Semitic peoples who would have inhabited the lands adjacent to the canal in modern day Sinai Peninsula, would have found it to be the centre of a huge opportunity for trade. In fact, for the Hyksos tribes, achieving control over the canal may have been paramount in order to fulfil their ambitions. Indeed, the Semitic Hyksos are believed to have ruled northern Egypt around the 17th century BCE from the city of Avaris, its remnants found in the Tell el-Dab'a archaeological site in the eastern region around the mouth of the Nile delta.

An interesting point to note, is that the archaeological site at Tell el-Dab'a has uncovered Minoan frescos believed to be from a period prior to the eruption of Thera circa 1600 BCE in the present-day Island of Santorini, due to the "lack of late Minoan finds" (Matić, 2014: 282) in Tell el-Dab'a. Therefore, the Hyksos seat of power at Avaris demonstrates an aspect of cosmopolitanism. Moreover, its location on the eastern part of the Nile delta, may have through their cultural influence and knowledge of Egyptian hieroglyphs contributed to the eventual creation of the Canaanite/Phoenician proto-Sinaitic script that borrows from Egyptian hieroglyphs to create an abjad that suited the tribes' mother tongue and which later developed into what came to be known as Phoenician in one city-state and Hebrew in another.

With regards to "the date of the earliest of the proto-Sinaitic writings...the principal debate is between an early date, around 1850 BCE, and a late date, around 1550 BCE" (Simons, 2011: 24). This range coincides with the accepted dates for the Second Intermediate Period during which the 'Hyksos' are believed to have successfully invaded the Nile delta through attacks "by one or more Canaanite chieftains" (Ryholt, 1998: 303) during a time of political upheaval and famine. However, my understanding of the evidence is that this 'invasion' of Lower Egypt may have been a gradual process from a merchant class who rose to prominence and formed the elites of the XV Dynasty.

Moreover, it must be noted that the 'Hyksos' maintained their independence against the Egyptians due to their grasp of a military technology that had given the Hittites an advantage in Anatolia. Indeed, it was the technological advantage of the two-horse war chariot (Hernández, 2014: 109) or 'Merkava' that was imported into Lower Egypt during the Second Intermediate Period that may have allowed the Hyksos to maintain rule over Lower Egypt as the 15th dynasty circa 1630–1523 BCE. Indeed, it was the 'Hyksos' who are believed to have also introduced the technology of the composite bow to the northern African theatre of war (Hernández, 2014: 111), which at the time would have been the equivalent of introducing the stinger missile and armoured tank into a theatre of war dominated by muskets and horses.

Figure 21: Beni Hasan wall painting, ca. 1890 BCE. Hyksos with livestock

With this technological advantage, victory over the Hyksos under the Pharaoh Apepi or Apophis would have only been possible in a theatre of war where the Egyptians would manage to eliminate these advantages. In earlier battles during the Second Intermediate Period, there is no mention of the "use of chariots by Kamose in his campaigns against the Hyksos" (Hernández, 2014: 113), which may have ended in defeat. This changed under Pharaoh Ahmose I who continued the fight against the Hyksos. Accounts show that "Ahmose relied on an unknown, but very effective, number of chariots, which Kamose must have plundered in his campaigns against the Hyksos" (Hernández, 2014: 114). Moreover, Ahmose "attacked Hyksos cities by land and water" (Hernández, 2014: 114). A victory over the Hyksos by Ahmose I, is described in the text of the autobiography of Ahmose son of Ibana, in a battle that appears to have been open littoral or shoreline combat by Egyptian marines, which may have caught the Hyksos at Avaris by surprise and led to the destruction of the city and the enslavement of many Hyksos.

Figure 22: 1300 BCE Depicting road Connecting Egypt with Canaan

The Children of Ba'al

It may be plausible to surmise that the Hyksos who survived the fall of Avaris and were not enslaved by Ahmose I and his troops, may have fled eastwards to the Levant and joined the other Semitic tribes that lived there. Indeed, "the Phoenician language, Hebrew language, and all of their sister Canaanite languages were largely indistinguishable dialects" (Naveh, 1987: 101) at that time. The literacy, skillsets and expertise of these Hyksos refugees would have served to strengthen the Canaanite city states of Tyre, Sidon, Byblos and Beirut whose trade network would later spread across the Mediterranean in the Late Bronze Age. It is at this stage that we arrive at our next destination, the Phoenician Iberian Peninsula.

Much like Columbus is said to have 'encountered' the peoples of the New World, we can arguably infer that the Phoenicians would have 'encountered' the Neolithic peoples of the Iberian Peninsula like Calpeia when setting up their settlements in 'Cadiz' or 'Gadir'

(Punic: ꓘA⅂ꓘ) around 1100 BCE (Quinn, 2018: 116) or 'Malaga' or 'Malaka' (Punic: ꓘꓶ⅂ꟼ) circa 770 BCE. Indeed, as archaeologist Miriam Balmuth rightly states, "the task of those who [study] the prehistory of an area as evidently peripheral as the Iberian Peninsula [is] to document the arrival and spread of these advances on the basis of the similarities of archaeological assemblages" (Balmuth, 1997: xv).

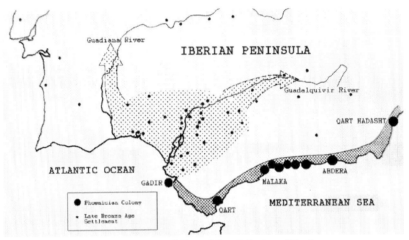

Figure 23: Map of Phoenician Colonies of Iberia

An interesting anecdote to mention, is that the city of Malaga may have got its name from the Phoenician word 'malakat' translated as a "place of passage" (Treumann-Watkins, 1992: 29), a faculty (Arabic: ملكات) or evidently, "from a Carthaginian word meaning the 'fish-processing place'" (Corcoran, 1963: 208), a necessary industry for the manufacture of Garum, a sought-after, umami flavoured, luxury product similar to the modern-day Worcestershire sauce, the product that is a staple in most

Venezuelan larders and is typically referred to as 'English sauce' by Venezuelans. In fact, if you are curious as to the taste of Carthaginian Garum, the University of Cadiz has released a product called 'Flor de Garum' based on their research on the ancient Roman Garum factory at the 'Baelo Claudia' archaeological site near Gibraltar, a practice which continued even into the time of Pliny the Elder (24-79 AD) who refers to the luxury mackerel garum made in New Carthage, Iberia as "exquisite liquid" (Corcoran, 1963: 204).

The origins to these ancient settlements of southern Spain should serve to demonstrate that the Late Bronze Age and later history surrounding the cultures of Iberia cannot possibly be told without first discussing the influence of the Phoenicians and later the Carthaginians who have had a significant influence on its cultural development. Nevertheless, it must be noted that during Franco's regime, "professional opportunities for archaeologists were limited, and the ties of patronage correspondingly strong" (Balmuth, 1997: xv). In Miriam Balmuth's opinion, this top-down approach pre-1970s meant that "senior archaeologists were all normativists and were in a position to exclude dissidents" (Balmuth, 1997: xv) and findings that were outside of the accepted views at the time.

The devolution of administrative regulation and control over archaeological works that came with the death of Franco has provided a boom in archaeological interest since the 1970s. This freedom laid the foundations for archaeologist Robert Chapman's seminal work 'Emerging complexity' published in 1990 which sought to discuss with the new data made available since the 1970s, the story of Calpeia's pre-historic Spain. Indeed, we know from archaeological evidence like Calpeia and the 'Almagra' red ochre ceramics discussed earlier, that southern Iberia may have been settled from at least 5500 BCE, as discussed earlier in the book.

According to Josephine Quinn in her book 'In Search of the Phoenicians', the Phoenicians who may have encountered these Neolithic Iberians, "did not in fact exist as a self-conscious collective" (Quinn, 2018: xvii). However, it could be argued that in that case, no people truly exist as a collective, but rather form co-operatives based on shared values, culture, history and kinship that serves to bind them as a defined collective, despite and above their self-interest. Moreover, the author would agree with Ernest Gellner's theory of nationalism expressed in his book 'Nations and Nationalism' that "nationalism is not a sentiment expressed by pre-existing nations; rather it creates nations where they did not previously exist" (Gellner, 2006: xxv).

However, it may be more plausible to suggest that Gellner is only somewhat correct with his assumption regarding pre-existing nations. The Westphalian system of nations that emerged after 1648 did not invent 'nations', more than it codified the territorial boundaries of the Western European Kingdoms after the Thirty Years War. In this sense, we see how in spite of cultural differences, certain peoples are part of nations that fall outside of their cultural sphere. One modern example of this is the region of

South Tyrol, Italy, which is evidently culturally Germanic in all but name and nationality since 1919.

With this context of nationhood, cultural spheres and self-conscious collectives, we refer back to the Iberian mines at Tharsis or Tartessos, which are believed to have been situated near the modern Spanish city of Huelva, northwest of Cadiz. It is interesting to note that Tharsis is believed to be mentioned multiple times in the Old Testament as Tarshish (Treumann-Watkins, 1992: 29), with specific mention of its ships "bringing gold, silver, ivory" (2 Chronicles 9:21) to the heart of the Middle East, precisely to the vaults of King Solomon.

In Strabo's 'Geography', published around 7 BCE he refers to Phoenician Iberia as 'Turdetania' (Latin: Land of the Thrushes) and states that the original name for the Guadalquivir river, which the Romans called the Baetis, was the "Tartessus" (Strabo, 3.2.11). Whether the city was named after the river or vice versa, is unclear in the text, although he does mention the 'Sierra Morena' (Brunette Hills) which he calls the "Silver Mountain" (Strabo, 3.2.11) on account of its mineral wealth. The 'Sierra Morena' mountain range is known to have been "the most highly mineralised region known to the ancient world" (Rickard, 1928: 131). The city of Tartessos (Carpia) was eventually destroyed by Carthage about 510 BCE (Checkland 1967: 37) when it sought to consolidate its control over Iberia. It is at this point that the colony of 'Gadir' then became the furthest western Punic city of importance to the ancient world.

Hercules and Hades

As stated in an earlier chapter, Strabo mentions that 'Gadir' (Gades) and its adjoining islands were called 'Erytheia' (Strabo, Bk. 3, 2: 11). 'Erytheia' is commonly known as the place where the tenth labour of Hercules (Heracles) took place to obtain the cattle of the three-bodied giant Geryon. What is not commonly known is that the home of Hercules was the city of Tyre. Indeed, even from around 170 BCE it was still not uncommon to use a vast sum of "silver to pay for a sacrifice to the god Hercules" (II Mac. 4.19). In the case of the Jewish High Priest Jason (Hebrew: יאסון) he reportedly was willing to pay 22,500 pounds of silver, the modern cash equivalent today would be roughly £10 million, to the God Ba'al Melqart (Hercules). Suffice to say that it was not the only reason that the High Priest Jason was deemed unpopular by his people.

These Melqart (Hercules) tythes to Tyre were very important and even though the High Priest Jason's contribution was driven by a desire to participate in the Quadrennial Games, that were being held in Tyre at the time, it nevertheless demonstrates his understanding of one aspect of the Tyrian spring ritual central to the Ba'al cycle, a story that has been brought to life by the many modern translations of the Ugaritic clay tablets KTU/CAT 1.1 - 1.6, like that of Professor Umberto Cassuto of the Hebrew University of Jerusalem .

Professor Cassuto describes Melqart's nemesis thus: "Mot has a constant natural longing to kill, to collect vast numbers of dead bodies and pile them up in enormous heaps which he then devours insatiably" (Cassuto, 1962: 80). To a modern ear Cassuto's description of Mot would sound like a personification of greed, which if left unchecked would eventually destroy the whole world. In the Ugaritic clay tablets, it specifically mentions that "it took Baal seven years to overcome Mot" (Cassuto, 1962: 79), which in fact sounds more like a metaphor for a drought than a mere changing of the seasons between "rainy winter and dry summer" (Cassuto, 1962: 77). In fact, the word 'Mot' (Hebrew: מֵתוּ) (Punic: X⅂ℳℸ) in modern Hebrew still used as the word for 'death' in the less threatening past tense.

However, unlike the Greek interpretation of Hercules and his final labour in Hades, in the 'Ba'al Cycle' it is not Ba'al Hadad (Melqart) who eventually triumphs over 'Mot', but rather his sister Anat, after he mistakenly brags about "how he found Baal and killed him" (Cassuto, 1962: 80). Anat, like the Goddess Ninḫursaĝ was to the Sumerians, is believed to have been "regarded as the Goddess of life" (Cassuto, 1962: 85) by the Canaanites. Therefore, it may be plausible to suggest that over the many centuries the Goddess Anat would eventually become known to Tunisians in the present day as 'Omek Tannou' (Arabic: طانقو أمك) or 'Mother Tanit' in the rainfall ritual still practiced in Tunisia. Also, one could argue that the modern flag of Tunisia (Fig. 24) holds an homage to the mother Goddess 'Tanit' at its centre, in that the five-pointed star and crescent moon (C⁎) hieroglyphs when placed together meant 'month' to the Ancient Egyptians (Gardiner, 1927: 486) and the calendar month is a figurative sign which denotes fertility in the divine feminine.

Figure 24: Flag of Tunisia adopted 20 October 1827

Bibliography

Adoum, O. A., Micheal, B. O., & Mohammad, I. S. (2012). Phytochemicals and hypoglycaemic effect of methanol stem-bark extract of Ficus sycomorus Linn (Moraceae) on alloxan induced diabetic Wistar albino rats. African Journal of Biotechnology, Vol.11 (17), pp.4095-4097.

Arteaga, O., Kölling, A., Kölling, M., Roos, A. M., Schulz, H., & Schulz, H. D. (2001). El puerto de Gadir. Investigación geoarqueológica en el casco antiguo de Cádiz, Rev. Atlántica-Mediterránea Prehist. Arqueol. Soc, vol.4, pp.345-416

Arteaga Matute, O., & Roos, A. M. (2002). El puerto fenicio-púnico de Gadir: una nueva visión desde la geoarqueología urbana de Cádiz. SPAL, 11, 21-39.

Assmann, J., & Lorton, D. (2005). Death and Salvation in Ancient Egypt. Cornell University Press.

Balmuth, M., Gilman, A., & Torreira, L. P. (Eds.). (1997). Encounters and transformations: the archaeology of Iberia in transition (Vol. 7). A&C Black.

Beckerath, J. V. (1958). Notes on the Viziers ʿAnkhu and ʾIymeru in the Thirteenth Egyptian Dynasty. Journal of Near Eastern Studies, 17(4), 263-268.

Bietak, M. (1991). Egypt and Canaan during the Middle Bronze Age. Bulletin of the American Schools of Oriental Research, 281(1), 27-72.

Breasted, J.H. (1916). Ancient Times: A History of the Early World. Boston et al.: Ginn and Co.

Carretero, M. I., Pozo, M., Gómez Toscano, F., Ruiz Muñoz, F., Abad de los Santos, M., González-Regalado Montero, M. L., ... & Silva, P. (2010). 'Primeras evidencias de contaminación histórica en el Parque Nacional de Doñana (SO de España)', Studia Geologica Salmanticensia, 46 (1): pp. 65-74

Cassuto, U. (1962). Baal and Mot in the Ugaritic Texts. Israel Exploration Journal, 12(2), 77-86.

Chapman, R., Chapman, C. R., & Renfrew, C. (1990). Emerging complexity: The later prehistory of south-east Spain, Iberia and the west Mediterranean. Cambridge et al.: Cambridge University Press.

Checkland, S. G. (1967). The Mines of Tharsis: Roman, French and British Enterprise in Spain (Vol. 10). London, Allen, pp.36-40

Collins, S. (2010). Catching Fire (Hunger Games, Book Two). Scholastic Inc.

Corcoran, T. (1963). Roman Fish Sauces. The Classical Journal, 58(5), 204-210.

Drewal, H. (1988). Performing the Other: Mami Wata Worship in Africa. TDR (1988-), 32(2), 160-185. doi:10.2307/1145857

Drewal, H. J. (2008). "Introduction: Charting the Voyage". In Drewal, Henry John (ed.). Sacred Waters: Arts for Mami Wata and other divinities in Africa and the diaspora. Bloomington: Indiana University Press.

Finkelstein, I., & Silberman, N.A. (2002) The Bible Unearthed. New York et al.: Simon & Shuster

Gardiner, A.H. (1927) Egyptian Grammar: Being an Introduction to the Study of Hieroglyphs, London: Clarendon Press

Gellner, E. (2006). Nations and Nationalism. Oxford: Blackwell Publishing.

Goedicke, H. (1984). Abi-Sha (i)'s Representation in Beni Hasan. Journal of the American Research Center in Egypt, 21, 203-210.

Harrison, R. J. (1988). Spain at the Dawn of History: Iberians, Phoenicians, and Greeks. Thames and Hudson.

Hernández, R. (2014). The Role of the War Chariot in the Formation of the Egyptian Empire in the Early 18 th Dynasty. Studien Zur Altägyptischen Kultur, 43, 109-122.

Hoffmeier, J. K. (2005) Ancient Israel In Sinai: The Evidence for the Authenticity of the Wilderness Tradition, Oxford University Press

Huntington, S.P. (1993). The clash of civilizations. Foreign affairs, 72(3), 22-49.

Josèphe, F. (2000). Flavius Josephus: Translation and Commentary, Volume 10: Against Apion (Vol. 10). Brill.

Karangi, M. M. (2005). The Sacred Mugumo Tree: Revisiting the roots of Gikuyu cosmology and worship: A case study of the Gicugu Gikuyu of Kirinyaga District in Kenya (Doctoral dissertation, SOAS University of London).

Keel, O. (1992). Das Recht der Bilder gesehen zu werden: Drei Fallstudien zur Methode der Interpretation altorientalishcer Bilder. Freiburg and Universitätsverlag/Göttingen: Vandenhoeck & Ruprecht

Mailhammer, R., & Vennemann, T. (2019). The Carthaginian North: Semitic influence on early Germanic: A linguistic and cultural study (Vol. 32). John Benjamins Publishing Company.

Matić, U. (2014). "MINOANS", kftjw AND THE "ISLANDS IN THE MIDDLE OF w3ḏ wr" BEYOND ETHNICITY. Ägypten Und Levante / Egypt and the Levant, 24, 275-292.

Meltzer, E. S. (2004). "Sinuhe, Jonah and Joseph: Ancient 'Far Travellers' and the Power of God", in: Ellens, J. H. et al. (eds.), God's Word for Our World, vol. II. Theological and Cultural Studies in Honor of Simon John De Vries (London-New York: Clark/Continuum), 77-81.

Naveh, J. (1987), "Proto-Canaanite, Archaic Greek, and the Script of the Aramaic Text on the Tell Fakhariyah Statue", in Miller; et al. (eds.), Ancient Israelite Religion, Philadelphia: Fortress Press, pp.101-114.

Padilla-Monge, A. (2016). Huelva y el inicio de la colonización fenicia de la Península Ibérica. Pyrenae, 47(1), 95-117.

Quinn, J. (2018). In search of the Phoenicians. Princeton et al.: Princeton University Press.

Renfrew, C. (1987), Archaeology and language: the puzzle of Indo-European origins. London: Jonathan Cape.

Rickard, T. (1928). The Mining of the Romans in Spain. The Journal of Roman Studies, 18, 129-143. doi:10.2307/296070

Ryholt, K. S., & Bülow-Jacobsen, A. (1998). The Political Situation in Egypt during the Second Intermediate Period, c. 1800-1550 BC (Vol. 20). Museum Tusculanum Press.

Schulman, A. R. (1980). Chariots, Chariotry and the Hyksos. Journal of the Society for the Study of Egyptian Antiquities 10.2, pp. 105–53.

Simons, F. (2011). Proto-Sinaitic – Progenitor of the Alphabet, Rosetta 9, pp.16-40.

Shanahan, M. (2016). Gods, Wasps and Stranglers: The Secret History and Redemptive Future of Fig Trees. Chelsea Green Publishing.

Strabo (1923). Geography, Volume II: Books 3-5. Translated by Horace Leonard Jones. Loeb Classical Library 50. Cambridge, MA: Harvard University Press.

Tappan, E.M. ed., (1914) The World's Story: A History of the World in Story, Song and Are, Vol. III: Egypt, Africa, and Arabia, trans. W. K. Flinders Petrie, Boston: Houghton Mifflin, pp. 41-46.

Treumann-Watkins, B. (1992). Phoenicians in Spain. The Biblical Archaeologist, 55(1), 29-35.

Turchin, P. (2007). War and peace and war: The rise and fall of empires. New York: Penguin Group.

Chapter Six

From Carthage with Love

"So farewell hope, and with hope farewell fear, Farewell remorse: all good to me is lost; Evil, be thou my good" —

John Milton, Paradise Lost, IV, l. 108

Phoenician Iberia

At the end of the 'Ba'al Cycle', Melqart (Hercules) and Mot (Death) are both resurrected, and their conflict begins anew in a never-ending war between "rainy winter and dry summer" (Cassuto, 1962: 77). Indeed, much like the Egyptian God Osiris, 'Ba'al Melqart' (Punic: 𐤗𐤀𐤐𐤋𐤌 𐤋𐤏𐤔), which translates as 'Lord King of the City', also known as 'Ba'al Hadad' (Ugaritic: 𐎁𐎍), the storm God, was a resurrecting God of the harvest and spring, as well as a protector of sailors. In the spring he would die and be born again to jubilant celebrations in Tyre and other Phoenician colonies, where palm branches may have been used as a gift to celebrate Melqart's victory over death (Ziemann, 2015: 10), in a similar fashion to the modern celebrations of Palm Sunday at Easter.

The 'Ba'al Cycle' perhaps shows us that famine and death was one of the many real concerns that worried the people of Tyre. To alleviate this worry, the Phoenicians indulged in what sociologist Émile Durkheim called a "cult of personality" (Lehmann 2013:

115), demonstrating an "exaltation of human personality" (Lehmann 2013: 115) and "the glorification not of the self but of the individual in general" (Lehmann 2013: 115). As such, Melqart and Tanit were the embodiments of the personality traits and characteristics this ancient society may have glorified in the individual. In Erytheia especially, an island at the furthest western point of the known world in ancient times, identified by the ancient Greeks as one of the 'Hesperides Islands' (also known as the *Atlantides*), upon which was built the Phoenician colony of Gadir (Cadiz), a temple honouring Melqart would have been found there.

Moreover, it is also at this most western point of the ancient world that we find the pillars of Melqart, an ancient symbol that marked the edge of civilization. Since about 550 BCE, the time of Herodotus, known in the west as the 'father of history', the link between the pillars of Melqart at Gadir and Hercules has been "beyond question" (Burkert, 1985: 210). In modern times, the pillars of Melqart are more commonly known as the Pillars of Hercules, the closest two points between southern Europe and northern Africa. It is believed that a pyre would be lit in Gadir every spring, as part of a fire festival, to mark the rebirth or 'egersis' (resurrection) of Melqart, who would rise from the ashes.

It is curious to note at this point, that the Greek word 'phoinix', is not only used to mean 'palm trees' and 'Phoenicians' but is also used to describe the colour of deep purple. Indeed, this cloth of Kings, a luxury item the Phoenicians were well known for producing in the ancient world, was deep purple coloured cloth.

Therefore, a 'phoinix' festival could have been an apt manner to describe a celebration that involves the resurrection of a God who rises out of the ashes after having been plunged into a fiery pyre. Our modern phoenix metaphor, which has been passed down to us from Greek folklore may have been developed from an observation of this fire festival ritual, coupled with the Ancient Egyptian myth of the god Bennu (𓅣) a Heron deity whose name is related to the verb 'weben' which literally means "to rise" (Wilkinson, 2003: 212).

The Greeks may have come across this fire festival honouring Melqart at Mount Oita south of Thermopylae, where "every four years a fire festival was celebrated there with ox sacrifices and agones" (Burkert, 1985: 210). In ancient Greece, 'agones' (Greek: Ἀγῶνες) meant a contest, specifically an athletics contest that takes place during a public celebration, much like the 'Funeral Games in Honour of Patroclus' described in Homer's 'Iliad' (Homer, Il. 6: 285) we discussed in chapter four. The significance of these fire festival games or 'agones' taking place at Mount Oeta, is that it is the place where Hercules is said to have died on a pyre, according to the Greek myth promoted by the tragedy 'The Women of Trachis' written by Sophocles and performed for the first time circa 450 BCE.

The motivation for performing a tragedy about Hercules after the Peloponnesian War may have been a political one. The Spartan royal lines of the Agiads and Eurypontids claimed to be descendants of Hercules and therefore, may have viewed Mount

131

Oita as a holy place, a claim that sounds absurd until one realises that it would not be unreasonable to suggest that the people of Sparta could have been of Semitic origin and sons of Melqart. In fact, a Semitic Sparta is described in the second book of Maccabees, when Jason flees the wrath of his people. In the Second book of Maccabees it is written, "he fled…to Greece, hoping to find refuge among the Spartans, who were related to the Jews" (II Mac. 5.9). Moreover, this claim over Mount Oita appears also to have extended over Mount Trachis, south west of Thermopylae, as well, since in 426 BCE it was conquered by Sparta and became a Spartan colony named Heraclea Trachinia. Thus, it appears that the highly defensible position of Mount Oita, southwest of Thermopylae would have been the ideal place for the nocturnal ritual practices of fire festivals that took place from the 6th century BCE onwards (Shapiro, 1983: 15).

In 'Greek Hero Cults and Ideas of Immortality' (1921), Professor L. R. Farnell discusses the notion that "the myth of Herakles' death on the funeral pyre on Mount Oeta was inspired by a Near Eastern ritual involving a divinity who, phoenix-like, dies in a fire and is reborn" (Shapiro, 1983: 15). As stated earlier, this divinity may have been Melqart, and its source, the city of Tyre. Included as part of these Melqart fire ceremonies, especially those that took place in Carthage, seems to have been an element of child sacrifice "in honour of the sons of the strong the 'Alkeidai'" (Burkert, 1985: 210).

However controversial and barbaric this ritual may sound to us, one must appreciate, without prejudice or our own moral values, that in the eyes of the practitioners of these Melqart rituals "Heracles ascends through the flames to the Gods" (Burkert, 1985: 210). Indeed, in this respect, "...there was probably also a notion of fire as a purifying agent" (Shapiro, 1983: 16), which meant that the ritual may have served as a more fatal form of blessing or baptism. In fact, in the Homeric 'Hymn to Demeter', in line 239 it is written, "the goddess roasts the baby Demophon in a fire to make him immortal" (Shapiro, 1983: 16).

It is within this context that we can discuss the 'tophets' found in Tunisia (Quinn, 2018: 161) sensibly, not to suggest barbarism or that life was cheap in the ancient world, but rather to state that it is a logical extension of an ancient culture that venerates fire as a sacred and holy purifier. Apotheosis and its association with sacrifice is still with us in modern times, the most practiced of these sacrifice rituals is that of Easter, where Christian practitioners remember the painful sacrifice of Jesus Christ on the cross, where his death served to wash away the sins of the world. Luckily for Christians, water was perhaps a less painful and physically harmful symbol for purity and holiness.

Nevertheless, while Christianity sought to adopt water as its more passive signifier, its practitioners in Venezuela have sometimes opted to re-enact the Passion of Christ, in all its gory detail. Moreover, Christians in Spain and Venezuela still practice and wish to be spectators in the art of bull fighting, where the red mantle of the matador, signifies the fire that, with each crossing, draws the bull closer to its maker. Apotheosis, in the case of this particular 'Ba'al Cycle' ritual, is gained by the matador, a title which literally means 'killer' in Spanish, and who is arguably the personification of Mot (Death). Therefore, it is Mot rather than the Bull who becomes the Hercules, "the hero who is always strong, never defeated and exceptionally [virile]" (Burkert, 1985: 210).

The relative ease at which Tyre was able to operate freely and expand after the Bronze Age collapse circa 1177 BCE, may have principally been due to the relative weakness and disarray of its rivals during the period following the Bronze Age collapse, which allowed the Phoenicians to establish strongholds as far west as Cadiz. Moreover, in Spain, archaeological evidence points to the local worship of Melqart (Heracles) in Andalusia, referred to as Ba'al (Punic: 𐤋𐤏𐤁), the Phoenician word for 'Lord', in a sign of respect and subservience. We have discussed how in Sparta, the Agiad and Eurypontid royal lineages claimed to be the descendants of Heracles who supposedly conquered Sparta after the Bronze Age collapse. Around this time, we are told by the Historian Josephus that the King of Tyre Hiram I, a contemporary of King David and his son King Solomon, created the Great Temple of Melqart in Tyre, as well as helped with the construction of the First Temple in the Kingdom of Israel (Punic: 𐤋𐤀𐤓𐤔𐤉) in Jerusalem, completed circa 960 BCE.

Temples to Melqart

The population expansion and prosperity described in the historical evidence also finds parallels in the Y-chromosome genetic record. With the advent of the technology of metallurgy, the J2 paternal lineage is believed to have migrated south and west from the southern Caucasus towards Mesopotamia and the Levant (Palumbi, 2016: 6). The J2 Y-haplogroup could then have migrated and propagated in Anatolia and the Eastern Mediterranean with the advent of civilizations following the Bronze Age collapse (Hughey et al., 2013: 4).

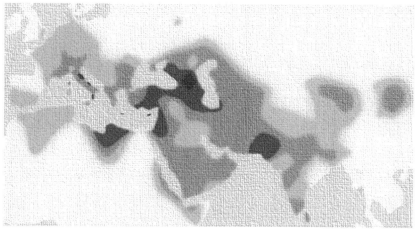

Figure 25: Map of Y-Haplogroup J2 Distribution and Density Mao of Africa, Asia and Europe
based on International Society of Genetic Genealogy (ISOGG) data

Indeed, it must be noted that "although the phylogeography of haplogroup J is complex, its radiation seems to be concentrated mainly in the Bronze Age, an essential period for the establishment of the modern European genetic pool" (Ferragut, 2020: 6). Moreover, the branch J2-M172 has "its high frequencies in the Levant and is the most frequent sub-haplogroup in Europe, mainly throughout the Mediterranean basin" (Ferragut, 2020: 6). In fact, this genetic evidence can serve as signs of Phoenician maritime migrations to the west, as "the Phoenicians have been linked to J2 and also to the other main branch, J1-M267" (Ferragut, 2020: 6). The lineage J1-M267 "has its maximum frequency in Arabia, but also high frequencies in the Middle East and in Jewish groups" (Ferragut, 2020: 6).

What is made clear from the map in Fig.25 is that a vast number of the ancient Middle Eastern and Mediterranean civilisations flourished in territories where J2 lineages were preponderant. The Assyrians, Etruscans, Israelites, Greeks, Hattians, Hurrians, Minoans, Persians, Phoenicians (Carthaginian colonies), and to a smaller extent due to the Etruscans, the Romans, are all civilizations descended from J2 lineages. Indeed, all of the seafaring civilisations that flourished after the Bronze age collapse were predominantly formed by men from a J2 lineage and coincides with the belief held by some academics that "the Phoenicians spoke a language that does not belong to the Indo-European group of northern Europe but rather the Semitic group, along with Hebrew, Babylonian and Assyrian" (Renfrew 1987: 46). Moreover, we note that another distinct characteristic of the J2 male is the preponderance of cattle worship in their rituals.

In the Neolithic sites of Çatalhöyük and Alaca Höyük found in central Anatolia, we find the oldest evidence of bull worship and a preponderance of Goddess worship (Mellaart, 1967: 181). We find bulls depicted in Minoan frescos and in ceramics found in Crete and in Cyprus we find bull-horned altars made of stone and also terracotta figurines with bull-masks. The Babylonians, Canaanites, Carthaginians, Hattians and Sumerians all had bull deities and as discussed earlier in this chapter, the ritual of dodging the charge of a bull which still forms part of Venezuelan, Spanish and French traditions and is found in the Andalusian region of southern Spain (home to the city of Cadiz) and the Provence region of southern France to this day, are two regions with a high number of males from J2 lineages. Therefore, it may come as no surprise that other civilizations with a high preponderance of J2 males also shared a tradition of bull leaping. For example, in the Achaemenid civilization of Bactria (Persia), the Hittite civilization of Anatolia, the Minoan civilization of Crete, the Indus Valley civilization in India and in Egypt, the Levant and Syria (Van Dijk, 2013: 144).

Although the civilizations of the Levant shared a common ancestry, it appears that the Arabic proverb that "blood is thicker than milk" (Turnbull, 1898: 10), seems to hold true in that each civilization held each other as a rival. Furthermore, there is an English proverb that warns 'do not put all your eggs in one basket' and when it comes to investing savings, the most prudent of financial planners have a tendency to present this idea as part of the logic behind a 'diversified portfolio'. Indeed, historical and archaeological evidence demonstrates that Tyre seems to have adopted this approach around 820 BCE to manage their risk to piracy and attacks from rival fleets, who sought to gain the raw materials from their mining operations in Iberia and the island of Thasos, in the Mediterranean, carried by Phoenician flotillas.

In fact, despite the bad press expressed in Biblical stories against the Omirides Dynasty and its alliance with the Phoenicians, an alliance consecrated by Israelite King Ahab's marriage to princess Jezebel the daughter of King Ethbaal I (Punic: LO𐤔X) who reigned over Greater Lebanon from the City of Tyre from circa 868-836 BCE, "a brilliant stroke of international diplomacy"(Finkelstein et al, 2002: 169) and a union which may have brought peace between the two rival Kingdoms until the murder of Jezebel by a rival faction to King Ahab, Phoenicia continued to grow prosperous and influential even after Ethbaal's reign.

The Ethbaal Dynasty of Tyre

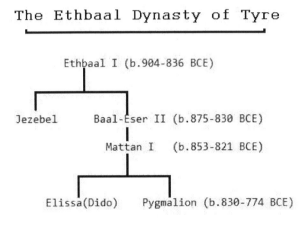

Source: Josephus, 'Against Apion' Book I.18

Figure 26: Progeny of the Rulers of Tyre & Greater Lebanon

Nevertheless, this activity and accumulation of wealth may have begun to attract unwanted attention from their political rivals in the region and we can presume that to mitigate the losses from piracy and perhaps any openly aggressive acts from its political rivals, establishing a sister colony in Carthage, in modern-day Tunisia, midway between the ports of Gadir in Iberia and Tyre in the Levant, would have made strategic sense to the King of Tyre Pygmalion (Punic: 𐤐𐤌𐤉𐤉𐤋𐤊). The Nora Stone, discovered in Sardinia and written in a Punic Semitic script is believed to have been created during the reign of Pygmalion of Tyre, who according to Josephus was crowned King at the age of nine and reigned circa 821-774 BCE.

Figure 27: Sketch of Nora Stone 9th Century B.C., Museo Archeologico Nazionale, Cagliari, Sardinia

What is curious about the Nora Stone artefact (sketched in Fig.27) is that both the Hebrew Language professor Frank Moore Cross and Middle Eastern Civilizations professor Brian Peckham translate the symbols on the top line, read from right to left as modern-day Arabic and Hebrew is read, as the phrase 'In Tarshish' (Punic: WW٩⊗ꟻ) (Hebrew: בתרשש) read phonetically as *btršš* and Hellenized as 'Tartessos' (Tharsis) or perhaps even the island of Thasos, as both places are known for having mines operated by the Phoenicians (Herodotus, 6.47). According to Herodotus, in Thasos he "found a temple of Heracles built by the Phoenicians, who made a settlement there when they voyaged in search of Europe; [constructed] as much as five generations before the birth of Heracles the son of Amphitryon in Hellas" (Herodotus, 2.44.4).

A further point to note about these religious temples to Melqart is that they appear to amalgamate four ancient cults into one. The first, is a cult of 'bull worship', which we discussed earlier in this chapter in relation to the 'Ba'al cycle'. The second, is a 'cult of the dead King', which mirrors the cult of the Pharoah observed in ancient Egypt, as Melqart was venerated as "the first mythical King of Tyre and ancestor of its Royal lineage" (Quinn, 2018: 121) and Melqart's relics were the first part of a trifecta of items that were used to establish a new colony. The third, is a 'cult of tree worship', which mirrors the cult of Hathor in Egypt as a 'mother goddess' and the 'Lady of the Sycamore' (Keel, 1992: 86-87). In the case of the Phoenicians and later the Carthaginians the expression of this cult was to use an olive tree as the second in a trifecta of "sacred objects...for the foundation of a new colony" (Quinn, 2018: 118).

The fourth cult is that of a combined 'Ba'al Cycle' and Exodus. The 'Ba'al Cycle' being the cult of the eternal flame versus the life-giving water, which mirrors the Persian Zoroastrian belief of fire as a purifier (Boyce, 1975: 455) and the Christian belief of water as a purifier and giver of life, represented in the eternal conflict between Mot (Death) and Melqart described in the 'Ba'al Cycle' and celebrated by the Phoenicians. This myth, amalgamated with a story of Exodus, presumably of the Hyksos wandering out of Egypt after their defeat at Avaris, is described in the book of Exodus as "by day the Lord went ahead of them in a pillar of cloud to guide them on their way and by night in a pillar of fire to give them light, so that they could travel by day or night" (Exodus 13:21).

According to Herodotus, around the Mediterranean, at the entrance of the Temples dedicated to Melqart stood "two pillars, one of refined gold, one of emerald: a great pillar that shone at night" (Herodotus, 2.44.2). If we go by the account in Exodus Thirteen, the golden pillar may have represented the pillar of fire that served as a metaphor for the lantern that guided a nomadic people in the darkness. Conversely, the emerald green pillar perhaps represented the pillar of cloud that guided them to a place with abundant precipitation and green pastures.

In his Pulitzer prize winning book 'God: A Biography' Jack Miles suggests that the pillars of fire and clouds in Exodus may instead suggest that the Semitic peoples who inspired the story of Exodus may have worshipped a volcano (Miles, 1995: 110). However, based on the archaeological, historical and DNA evidence that exists of the Semitic peoples of the Levant, the suggestion of a 'volcano cult' seems an unlikely conclusion to draw as there are no volcanoes in the coastal area from Lebanon to Egypt. Moreover, the fact that the God Melqart was also known as 'Ba'al Hadad' (Ugaritic: 𐎁𐎍), the storm God and a resurrecting God of the harvest and spring, it seems more likely that an emerald pillar would represent life and fertility rather than a plume of smoke. As any avid sailor will tell you, reading the clouds is a very useful skill to have if you want to find out what weather is heading your way.

The pillars may have served as a physical reminder of a belief in a spiritual dualism between, the insatiable God of Death (Mot) and the storm God (Hadad) that may have been a central tenant of Phoenician religious dogma. Certainly, a visiting pilgrim would first have to pass between the two pillars to enter the place where the central chamber of worship was found. However, an alternative suggestion begins with the etymology of the word 'Jerusalem' (Hebrew: שלמירו). Professor Sayce constructs the argument that the suffix SH-L-M (Hebrew: שְׁלם), means 'peace' (Hebrew: שׁוּלם) and refers to the El-Amarna Letters where 'Jerusalem' is said to appear in line 289.29 as 'URU ú-ru-sa-lim' "king of (the city of) Salim" (Sayce, 1911: 228).

Unfortunately, there is a problem with Professor Sayce's 'city of peace' argument in that it stems from his mistranslation and misunderstanding of the word 'Shalim'. Even in modern written Hebrew, there is a difference between 'Shalim' (Hebrew: שְׁלם), which means 'wholeness' or 'completeness' and 'shalom' which means 'peace'. In this context, the 'city of peace' becomes the 'city of wholeness' or more literally, the city of 'Shalim'. In the Canaanite pantheon of Gods, 'Shalim' was the 'evening star' in the sky and associated with Venus at dusk. As stated in chapter five, Venus has a 'green-flash effect' as the sun sets at dusk, the emerald green colour used by Herodotus to describe one of the Pillars of Melqart.

The significance of the second pillar of light, becomes obvious once we begin to accept that the emerald green pillar represents the Canaanite God 'Shalim'. In the Ugaritic text 'The Birth of the Gracious Gods', the God El "impregnates two women who in turn give birth to the dawn and dusk" (Bercerra, 2008: 51), the Gods 'Shahar' (Hebrew: שׁ.ח.ר) and 'Shalim' (Hebrew: םׁ.לׁשׁ) respectively. In modern Hebrew the word 'Shahar' is still used as a word for 'dawn' and in the old testament, specifically, Isaiah 14:12 the word is used to say "O light bringer, son of the dawn". In English Protestant Bibles like the one printed by the British and Foreign Bible Society, they use the word 'Lucifer' from the Latin for 'light bringer', 'Luciferos', to denote the light bringer as the morning star, the planet Venus in the night sky.

Venus, the morning star or lantern in the sky, may have been represented in the second Pillar of Melqart described by Herodotus as made of gold, due to the bright golden shine of the morning star in the morning dawn. The allegory of the twin pillars adds to the previously discussed importance that the Phoenicians may have placed on Venus, not only as Aštart (another name for the Goddess Shahar) of the two stages of the planet Venus in the night sky to mark the beginning and end of each day, denoted in Hebrew as Yom (Hebrew: יוֹם). The fact that Yom is also used in the Jewish Scriptures to denote 'time', will not be discussed in this book, only to state briefly that daylight, time and eternity were clearly important concepts that may have played a part in the ancient religious rituals of the peoples of the Levant, and to this day still are, as is the case in the new moon atonement periods of Lent, Ramadan (Arabic: رَمَضَان) and the month of Elul that culminates with the 'Day of Atonement' or Yom Kippur (Hebrew: כ. יפּוּר יוֹם.)

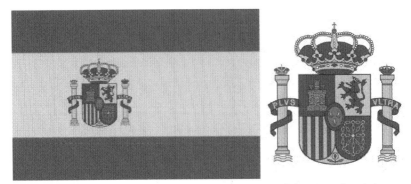

Figure 28: J.B. Modern Flag of Spain. The current design of the King of Spain's Coat of Arms was created in 1981 but retains the Pillars of Hercules and the motto Plus Ultra (Further Beyond).

The importance of Venus to the Phoenician calendar and development of mathematics in the ancient should not be underestimated. Indeed, its importance became apparent on July 10, 2020, a few days after an important family celebration, when Venus was shining double as brightly as it usually does near the star Aldebaran, the eye of the constellation Taurus. This event, called 'the greatest illuminated extent' is part of a celestial pattern called 'the pentagram of Venus'. In each eight-year cycle, the planet Venus repeats each celestial phenomenon five times. Therefore, every eight years we witness five 'inferior conjunctions' as Venus passes between us and the sun and five 'superior conjunctions' as Venus passes the far side of the sun. Roughly thirty-six days before and later after an 'inferior conjunction' we witness, like clockwork, 'the greatest illuminated extent' of Venus as it passes 'perigee', the point when it is closest to earth and shining its brightest. In short, during each eight-year cycle a five-pointed star is drawn in the sky.

Figure 29: The 'pentagram of Venus' in James Ferguson. 1799. Astronomy Explained Upon Sir Isaac Newton's Principles (Plate 3)

A curious fact is that the deification of the planet Venus finds a parallel in Mesoamerican Mayan culture. The Mayan God 'No Ek' (Venus) is represented by a pictogram of a four-pointed star on the Chichén Itzá, a slight variant of the ancient Egyptian depiction of Venus as a hieroglyph of a five-pointed star. Nevertheless, much like in the 'Ba'al Cycle', the planet Venus whether in the form of the Goddess Anat, Aštart or the God No Ek, "the extreme declinations of Venus as [a] morning star were always attained...between late June and August" (Šprajc, 1993 :21) and Venus "was visible as an evening star...always some time before the [summer and winter] solstices: between April and June

145

(northerly extremes) and between October and December (southerly extremes)" (Šprajc, 1993 :21). When "viewed in the light of rainfall data…. the evening star extremes…approximately coincide with the start (northerly extremes) and with the end (southerly extremes) of the rainy season" (Šprajc, 1993 :21). This may serve to explain the pillar of clouds metaphor and its association with the 'evening star'.

Moving past the two pillars of Hercules, an account written by the Roman politician Silius Italicus in his epic poem 'Punica', written circa 28 AD, can help us picture what lay inside of the Phoenician Temple of Melqart in Gadir. He writes that it was built from wooden timbers that "never decayed" (Silius, 3.14-60, 115) and that in the Temple's central chamber, past the two gleaming pillars at the entrance was an "olive tree that symbolised the God [Melqart], as well as his bones" (Quinn, 2018: 117) (Silius, 3.14-60, 113). Alongside the olive tree, the Greek Geographer Pausanias describes that there were detailed reliefs of Melqart's twelve labours carved "above the doors of the temple" (Pausanias, 5.10.9) and Silius adds that at the centre of the temple "the fires on the hearth-stones [kept] the altars alight perpetually" (Silius, 3.14-60, 115) and behind the lit altars stood a carved relief of Mount Oeta that shined with the light of the "sacred fires, and the flames carry the hero's soul up to Heaven" (Silius, 3.14-60, 117).

The atmosphere, vivid imagery and symbology would have imbued any pilgrim visiting the Temple of Melqart at Gadir with a sense of wonder and solemnity, which may have been the intention of its architects. Yet, despite the popularity of Melqart across the Mediterranean what remains uncertain is the cult to Tanit that has been found in the city of Carthage and whether it would have made its way to Iberia. This question will be explored in the next part.

The Dawn of Carthage

In his book 'The Hero with A Thousand Faces', Joseph Campbell surmised that the "prime function of mythology and rite [is] to supply the symbols that carry the human spirit forward, in counteraction to those constant human fantasies that tend to tie it back" (Campbell, 2008: 7). We can see his point when we read the 'Epic of Gilgamesh' written circa 2000 BCE, 'The Ba'al Cycle' dated to circa 1500 BCE and even in the 'Myth of Princess Dido' and the creation of the colony at Carthage. The complexity of this myth is one that leads us back into the territory of the Y-haplogroup J2, specifically, found in the male populations of Northern Italy and Tunisia.

In Virgil's epic poem, 'the Aeneid', Queen Elissa flees the city of Tyre and the tyranny of her brother Pygmalion to establish her own new city of 'Carthage' or Qart-Hadašt (Punic: 𐤒𐤓𐤕𐤇𐤃𐤔𐤕) (English: New City), according to Timaeus, around the year 814 BCE (Quinn, 2018: 114). Archaeological evidence supports Timaeus' claims as there appears to be no evidence of a Phoenician settlement in the location of Carthage prior to the ninth Century BCE. Nevertheless, when the Phoenicians established their colony at Carthage the Berbers were already established in the region as "farmers with a strong pastoral element in their economy and fairly elaborate cemeteries" (Brett, 1996: 16).

This Berber civilization that had been established in this region of north Africa for at least one thousand years prior to the arrival of the Phoenicians, may have contributed to the cultural development of the myth of Dido and the transformation of Aštart (Punic: ✗𐤀✗𐤅𐤏), "the Semitic goddess" (Barton, 1934: 304) into the Carthaginian Goddess Tanit. It is curious that Tanit's symbol, found carved in steles discovered in Carthage's tophets, appears to be a combination of an ancient Egyptian life or 'ankh' symbol (☥), crowned with the hieroglyph that denotes a moon (☾).

It is understood that it is no coincidence that "the ankh, the Egyptian symbol for life" (Schwabe et. al, 1982: 445) is the same shape of as a "thoracic vertebra of an ungulate" (Schwabe et. al, 1982: 445). According to Professor Schwabe in his article 'Egyptian Beliefs about the Bull's Spine', "[ancient] Egyptians believed that sperm was produced in the thoracic spine" (Schwabe et. al, 1982: 445). Which means that 'Tanit's symbol' may have been a combination of the divine masculine and the divine feminine. Indeed, historian George Barton suggests that an integral part of the establishment of Tanit is the Dido Myth. He suggests that the nickname given to Queen Elissa of 'Dido' may have come from the Semitic root 'dwd' (Hebrew: דוד), which denotes kinship and can be used to express 'love' (Hebrew: מִידוֹד) (Barton, 1934: 305) pronounced phonetically as 'dwdym'.

Moreover, it is possible that the noun 'dwdym' may have been Hellenized to become Dido. The tragic love story that is the 'Dido Myth', which begins with the murder of her husband by the hands of her brother the young King Pygmalion, would have contributed to the idea that Queen Elissa was a tragic figure, much like Juliet in Shakespeare's 'Romeo and Juliet', doomed to have her love taken away from her. In Virgil's version of the 'Dido Myth', the fates conspire so that Queen Elissa loses her two lovers, before being overtaken by a grief so great that she "builds a funeral pyre and, in front of her people, throws herself into the fire" (Masri, 2017: 94).

We can begin to see a Phoenician theme emerge between a gruesome and painful suicide upon a pyre, attaining apotheosis and entry into the Kingdom of Heaven. This tale of suffering, much like the twelve labours of Hercules, which may be said to have been a geocentric myth retelling the yearly journey of the sun traversing the twelve houses of the horoscope, may have been a Carthaginian effort to establish an independent religion centred around the Goddess Tanit, and using Melqart's familiar trope to help establish the myth in the imagination of its citizens.

Therefore, perhaps the Tanit and popular 'Dido Myth' was the start of a new city deity, and an attempt at a move away from the cultural influence of a political hegemony based at the city of Tyre and its religion centred around the cult of Melqart to which every citizen owed a contribution to. It is in this context, that 'Tanit's symbol' which appears to embrace both masculine and feminine qualities and is coupled with an association to a "tree-divinity"

(Barton, 1934: 305), a familiar myth that the native Berber tribes of North Africa may have felt comfortable to associate with and worship, has meant that the Goddess Tanit has stood the test of time as 'Omek Tannou' (Arabic: طانقو أمك) or 'Mother Tanit' in a rainfall ritual still being practiced in Tunisia in the present day.

Moreover, despite the fact that over two thousand eight hundred years have passed since the myth of Dido was created, in modern Tunisia, Queen "Elissa has become a national symbol" (Masri, 2017: 94), perhaps even a Tunisian strong feminist symbol in a country where women are proudly called the "Daughters of Dido" (Masri, 2017: 94). The promulgation of the 'Dido myth', especially since the 1970s may have promoted this distinct gender empowerment and a demand for greater rights that was fed into Tunisia's modern history, process of democratisation and current status as an "Arab spring success story" (Masri, 2017: 7) since 2014.

Tunisian national pride and a defined Tunisian national identity was promoted and gained international attention under the UNESCO campaign 'Save Carthage' during the 1970s (Quinn, 2018: 12). The promotion of a 'Carthaginian' national identity may have led to Tunisia being the most progressive of all the Arab countries ("Tunisian women free to marry non-Muslims," 2017). The 'children of Carthage' narrative, 'the Dido Myth' and 'Tanit's symbol' have all since been imbued with political meaning to act as a unifying force and become symbols that represent freedom and self-determination of a of a civil society against any perceived tyranny and have been turned into a narrative of progress and success in the face of adversity.

Figure 30: An artist's impression of Queen Elissa (Dido)

In the decades that followed the foundation of Phoenician colony at Carthage in 814 BCE, while the city of Carthage flourished, due to its ideal position to control the trade traversing the Mediterranean west to east, in stark contrast, the city of Tyre found itself increasingly vulnerable and under siege. Indeed, from 724 BCE onwards the city of Tyre found itself under siege from its rivals to the north. First by the Assyrians in 724 BCE, then in 586 BCE by the Babylonians, in 539 BCE by Cyrus the Great of Persia and finally in 332 BCE by the Macedonians led by Alexander the Great. It was the fall of Carthage to Alexander the Great that led to a new world order where the city of Carthage rose in importance above Tyre.

However, even before the destruction of Tyre at the hands of Alexander the Great, Carthage had been attempting to increase its influence over the western Mediterranean by occupying the island of 'Ebesus' (Ibiza) around 654 BCE and conquering the city of Tartessos (Carpia) on the most southern tip of Iberia around 510 BCE (Checkland 1967: 37). By then, the Phoenician city of Gadir had become the furthest western Punic city of importance to the ancient world. To mark the point before this transition between Phoenicia and Carthage, we read how the 6th century Hebrew prophet Ezekiel describes Tyre as a city that "dwells at the entrance to the sea, merchant of many peoples on many coastlands...Tarshish (Carpia) trafficked with you because of your great wealth of every kind; silver, iron, tin, and lead they exchanged for your wares" (Ezekiel, 27: 3, 12). Therefore, it is clear that Carthage appears to gain prominence around the time of Tyre's destruction in 332 BCE.

We see this clearly in Aristotle's 'Politics', written around 340 BCE, in that he takes the time to provide an analysis of Carthaginian society and values in a book that deals with the other great powers of his day. What is curious about Aristotle's analysis is that it provides us with a greater historical perspective of the Lionel Jane's assumptions about Spanish character and Castilian values, touched upon briefly earlier in this book. Specifically, his opinion that Spaniards have been imbued with the "very physical characteristics of... the [northern point of the Iberian] peninsula, and ...the physical characteristic of Castile" (Jane, 1966: 19). In fact, the Carthaginian attitudes described by Aristotle that wealth is more important than virtue (Jowett, 1885: 62) may help explain why, whilst countries like the United Kingdom eventually found Roman Law to be insufficient and as a result developed virtue-based equity laws, Spain, in particular maintained Roman Law and even to this day does not recognize trusts that do not serve the interests of a business entity.

Moreover, the idea that "the same person should hold many offices, which is a favourite practice among the Carthaginians" (Jowett, 1885: 62) and his assessment that it is the root cause of short-sighted practices that deviate from democracy "and inclines to oligarchy" (Jowett, 1885: 61) may serve to demonstrate that the current economic and intellectual stasis evident in modern day Latin America may emerge from an undeniably Castilian nature but has in origins in a Carthaginian Iberia. Perhaps this 'culture of oligarchy' may explain why democracy (Δημοκρατία) might be quite a difficult system to put into practice in Iberian cultures. Moreover, why Spain only as recently as the 1970s returned to democracy after the death of its dictator Franco and why Venezuela is still mired by an authoritarian regime that does not hold free and fair elections.

However, just because a culture might not lend itself perfectly to certain values, does not mean that a change in attitude is impossible. In fact, it was in a childhood dominated by these Phoenician values that the mathematician and pre-Socratic philosopher Thales of Miletus, one of the great thinkers of the ancient world, grew up in around 600 BCE (Herodotus, 1.170). Thales as a free thinker may have realised the corrupting influence of a 'fiery death cult', that invariably places death (Mot)

153

at the forefront of the Herculean apotheosis myth, has on society. He instead chose a life in Greece and adopted the mantra 'know thyself'. In his book 'Battling the Gods: Atheism in the Ancient World' Tim Whitmarsh notes that rather than fire, Thales regarded "water as the primal matter, and because 'thal' is the Phoenician word for moisture, his name may have derived from this circumstance." (Whitmarsh, 2016: 66). Indeed, as mentioned before, water serves as a medium for less brutal and more nurturing rituals than fire.

As Joseph Campbell said in his 1980s series 'The Power and the Myth' "all the gods, all the heavens, all the hells, are within you", perhaps unintentionally paraphrasing Thales' much simpler but enigmatic phrase 'Know Thyself'. Brutality and heroism may sometimes be indistinguishable, especially in the case of a 'just war', and it is this false heroism and "the deeds of myth [that] survive into modern times" (Campbell, 2008: 2). We see it in popular movie franchises like 'The Avengers' or 'The Justice League', perpetuating the myth that fire is the most effective purifier and route to apotheosis. In a world with Nuclear weapons that kind of thinking would ultimately lead to mutually assured destruction. Moreover, in this context, films like 'Logan's Run', 'The Hunger Games Series' and even the 'Harry Potter Series', tap into the ancient Phoenician rituals of child sacrifice, apotheosis and baptisms of fire that Thales may have attempted to mitigate and shift public opinion away from during his lifetime.

Thales' success in introducing 'water' as part of northern Mediterranean purification rituals, may demonstrate that one man with a revolutionary idea can make a huge difference and save lives. Moreover, it is inevitable in any power dynamic that violence begets more violence as we saw in the Royal lineage of Queen Elissa. Her great-grandfather Ethbaal I, according to Josephus came to the throne in 871 BCE, by plotting murder despite being a "priest of Astarte" (Whiston, 1737: I.18) and her brother Pygmalion followed in his footsteps by ordering the assassination of his elder sister's husband Zakarbaal high priest of Melqart and ruler of Byblos "in his seventh year on the throne" (Rohl, 2010: 554).

The Carthaginians, like their Phoenician forebears before them, built a reputation of being cheats and oath breakers (Silius, 3.14-60, 113). Moreover, their increasingly confrontational nature led to "Carthage's final destruction by the Romans in 146 BCE" (Quinn, 2018: xv). This increasingly confrontational nature can be correlated with the Carthaginian need to mint silver coins they called 'Sheqel' (Punic: ᛚφW) circa 410 BCE to pay for their military campaigns in the Mediterranean. This increased military expenditure did not serve to strengthen Carthage but rather bankrupted it.

Roman Turdetania

We will not be focusing on the First and Second Punic wars between Rome and Carthage or General Hannibal (Punic: LOᛓᛁᛞ), whose name meant 'Baal is Gracious', and his crossing of the Alps. We will only focus on the outcome of the conflict: the creation of the Roman province of Turdetania in southern Iberia after the final defeat of Carthage in 146 BCE. In this context, Queen Elissa's leap into the fire in Virgil's 'Aeneid' can be seen to provide a "a mythical backdrop for 100 years of war between Rome [Aeneid] and Carthage [Dido]" (Masri, 2017: 94) represented in the tragedy. Romulus the mythical founder of Rome is seen as "the grandson of Aeneas [the Trojan]" (Rohl, 2010: 581), making Aeneas the progenitor of Roman civilization.

Figure 31: A Carthaginian silver shekel, dated 237–227 BC.
On the left, the Punic god Melqart; the reverse is a man riding a war elephant.

Moreover, this bond between Carthage and Rome goes far deeper. It is important to note that in a study led by Dr Katrin Westner it was found that before the Punic Wars her study found that "Roman coins [were] made of silver from the same sources as the coinage issued by Greek cities in Italy and Sicily" (Goldschmidt Conference, 2017). However, from 209 BCE onwards, "the majority of Roman coins show geochemical signatures typical for Iberian silver" (Goldschmidt Conference, 2017). This led Dr Westner's team to conclude that "this massive influx of Iberian silver significantly changed Rome's economy, allowing it to

156

become the superpower of its day" (Goldschmidt Conference, 2017).

According to Jean-Benoît Nadeau, author of 'The Story of Spanish', "the story of Spanish...starts with Rome" (Nadeu et al., 2013: 10). Indeed, as previously discussed, although the Phoenician contribution to language and alphabet development in Iberia may have been vast, after the fall of Carthage and the subsequent millennia of Roman influence if we study the etymology of most Spanish words, it is clear that most of the words and expressions that are currently used in modern Castilian Spanish, the language of Spain and Venezuela, can be seen to have their roots firmly planted in Vulgar Latin. It is commonly accepted that Castilian Spanish is a Romance language that flourished from a mixture of Vulgar Latin and Celtic much like its cousins Catalan, Aragonese, Galician, Occitan, French, and Portuguese.

During the Roman Republic, the former territories of Carthaginian Iberia were first divided into the southern Roman province of 'Hispania Ulterior' (English: Further Spain) and eastern Roman province of 'Hispania Citerior' (English: Nearer Spain). In these two provinces the Romans would take over where the Carthaginians left off. In the city of Gadir, the Greek translation of Melqart, Heracles, would be Latinised to become Hercules the son of Jupiter. In Malaga, the Garum factories would continue and, in the Sierra Morena, and 'Nova Carthago' (Spanish: Cartagena) the silver mining would continue.

As Rome established greater control over the Iberian Peninsula it renamed its first two Provinces 'Hispania Baetica' and 'Hispania Tarraconensis'. The Romans then added a third province to the west and called it 'Lusitania' after the Celtic tribe the "Lusitani who were living on the nearer side of the Tagus River" (Orosius, 4.21). The Iberian Peninsula would be home to Rome's wealthiest provinces as described in 'A History, against the Pagans' compiled by Galician Paulus Orosius, a disciple of St Augustus, in the 5th Century AD and in his work, we notice various Phoenician, Celtic and Roman settlements in Iberia that surprisingly still match the regions and cities of Spain as we know them today.

Figure 32: Roman Map of Iberian Provinces and Roads

These place names are: 'Gades' (Cadiz); 'Gallecia' (Galicia); 'Astures' (Asturias); 'Hispania Baetica' (Andalucia); 'Augusta Emerita' (Merida); 'Corduba' (Cordoba); 'Autrigones' (Basque Country); 'Novo Carthago' (Murcia); 'Vaccaei' (Valladolid); 'Castra Legionis' (Leon); 'Tarraconensis' (Tarragona); 'Toletum' (Toledo);

'Lusitania' (Portugal), to name a few. Between these Phoenician, Roman and Celtic settlements the Roman military-built roads and bridges to connect the various settlements together, the first of which was the 'Via Herculea' also known as the 'Via Augusta' and when gold was discovered in Asturias the Ab Asturica Burdigalam, now known as the 'Way of St. James', was built to connect Asturias with the town of Burdigala (Bordeaux) in Aquitania.

The northern Iberian settlements were slowly assimilated into the Roman Republic after the fall of Carthage and later into the Roman Empire, which would eventually collapse in 476 AD. During this time of assimilation, these Celtiberian tribes contributed many words that are pronounced with a heavy r sound that has been associated with the Spanish 'double r' words like 'carro' (cart/car), 'barro' (mud) and 'correa' (belt). Moreover, we also find Celtic words that are pronounced with a 'heavy r' but are not written with a 'double r' like 'bruja' (witch), 'raya' (line) and 'izquierda' (left).   Likewise, the Celtic suffix '-briga', possibly pronounced with a heavy r sound and meaning "fortified place" (Lorrio et al., 2005: 187) can be seen in the place names of a plethora of Iberian settlements, for example Lacobriga (Lagos) and 'Conímbriga' (Coimbra).

These Celtic day to day words that found their way into Vulgar Latin and have remained a feature of all the Celtiberian Romance Languages.   Nevertheless, the focus remained on 'Hispania Baetica'. Strabo mentions that the "Turdetanians are ranked as the wisest of the Iberians; and they make use of an alphabet, and possess records of their ancient history, poems, and laws written

159

in verse that are six thousand years old, as they assert" (Strabo, 3.1.6). Therefore, we can see a distinction between the Celtic cultures of the north and the Phoenician cultures in the south. Strabo claims that the cultures in the south "completely changed over to the Roman mode of life; with most of the populace not even remembering their own language anymore" (Strabo, 3.2.15), but as stated earlier in the book, the culture of Phoenician Andalusia is very different to that found in Celtic Galicia.

Indeed, to this day the cultural differences between northern and southern Spain have led to a sub-genre of 'Galician jokes', intended to make fun of the intellect of the Celtic peoples from the north. The irony is that with the fall of Rome, the Celtiberian tribes were finally allowed to flourish and come into their own and form the myriad of Visigothic Kingdoms we will discuss in the next chapter. Rome's influence would remain in Iberia in the form of the Roman Catholic Church, a force that would unite the Celts against a common rival.

Bibliography

Anderson, R., & Anderson, R. C. (2003). A short history of the sailing ship. New York: Dover Publications.

Barton, G. (1934) Semitic and Hamitic Origins. Philadelphia: University of Pennsylvania Press; London: H. Milford: Oxford University Press.

Bercerra, D. (2008). El and the Birth of the Gracious Gods. Studia Antiqua, 6(1), 10, pp.51-56

Boyce, M (1975), 'On the Zoroastrian Temple Cult of Fire', Journal of the American Oriental Society, Journal of the American Oriental Society, Vol. 95, No. 3, 95 (3): 454–465, doi:10.2307/599356

Brett, M., & Fentress, E. (1996). The Berbers. Oxford, UK: Blackwell Publishers

Burkert, W. (1985). Greek religion. Cambridge, MA: Harvard University Press.

Campbell, J., & Moyers, B. (1988). The Power of Myth, ed. Betty Sue Flowers, New York:
Doubleday Publishing Group.

Checkland, S. G. (1967). The Mines of Tharsis: Roman, French and British Enterprise in Spain (Vol. 10). London, Allen, pp.36-40

Cross, F. (1972). An Interpretation of the Nora Stone. Bulletin of the American Schools of Oriental Research, (208), 13-19. doi:10.2307/1356374

Cruciani, F., La Fratta, R., Trombetta, B., Santolamazza, P., Sellitto, D., Colomb, E. B., ... & Moral, P. (2007). Tracing past human male movements in northern/eastern Africa and western Eurasia: new clues from Y-chromosomal haplogroups E-M78 and J-M12. Molecular biology and evolution, 24(6), 1300-1311.

Durkheim, E. (1974). Sociology and philosophy. Simon and Schuster.

Durkheim, E. (1915). The Elementary Forms of the religious life. Translated by Joseph Swain. London: George Allen & Unwin Ltd.

Feldman, A. (1945). Thoughts on Thales. The Classical Journal, 41(1), 4-6.

Fleming, W. B. (1915). The History of Tyre (Vol. 10). New York: Columbia University Press.

Goldschmidt Conference. (14 August 2017) "Analysis finds defeat of Hannibal 'written in the coins of the Roman Empire'." ScienceDaily. ScienceDaily.

Haber, M., Doumet-Serhal, C., Scheib, C., Xue, Y., Danecek, P., Mezzavilla, M., ... & Matisoo-Smith, E. (2017). Continuity and admixture in the last five millennia of Levantine history from ancient Canaanite and present-day Lebanese genome sequences. The American Journal of Human Genetics, 101(2), 274-282.

Herodotus, (1920). The Histories. With an English translation by A. D. Godley. Cambridge, MA: Harvard University Press.

Homer. (1924) The Iliad with an English Translation by A.T. Murray, Ph.D. in two volumes. Cambridge, MA., Harvard University Press; London, William Heinemann, Ltd.

Hughey, J., Paschou, P., Drineas, P. et al. (2013). A European population in Minoan Bronze Age Crete. Nat Commun 4, 1861. https://doi.org/10.1038/ncomms2871

Jane, C. (1966). Liberty and Despotism in Spanish America. Preface by Salvador de Madariaga. New York: Cooper Square Publishers.

Jowett, B. (Ed.). (1885). The Politics of Aristotle: Introduction and translation. Vol. 1. London: Clarendon Press.

Kiguradze, T., & Sagona, A. (2003). Origins of the Kura-Araxes Cultural Complex. In A. T. Smith & K.
Rubinson (Eds.), Archaeology in the Borderlands, Investigations in Caucasia and Beyond The Cotsen
Institute of Archaeology at UCLA, Los Angeles, (pp. 38–94).

Lehmann, J. M. (2013). Deconstructing Durkheim: a post-post structuralist critique. London and New York: Routledge.

Lorrio, A. J. and Zapatero, G. R. (2005) "The Celts in Iberia: An Overview," e-Keltoi: Journal of Interdisciplinary Celtic Studies: Vol. 6, Article 4, pp.167-254.

Mellaart, J. (1967). Catal Huyuk: A Neolithic Town in Anatolia. New York: McGraw-Hill.

Miles, J. (1995). God: A biography. New York: Knopf Doubleday Publishing Group.

Nadeau, J. B., & Barlow, J. (2013). The Story of Spanish. New York: St Martin's Press.

Oldenburg, U. (1969). The conflict between El and Ba'al in Canaanite religion (Vol. 3). Leiden: E.J. Brill.

Orosius, P. (2010). Seven books of history against the pagans (Vol. 54). Liverpool: Liverpool University Press.

Palumbi, G. (2016). The Early Bronze Age of the Southern Caucasus. Oxford Handbooks Online. Oxford: Oxford University Press

Pausanias. (1918). Pausanias Description of Greece with an English Translation by W.H.S. Jones, Litt.D., and H.A. Ormerod, M.A., in 4 Volumes. Cambridge, MA, Harvard University Press; London, William Heinemann Ltd.

Peckham, B. (1972). The Nora Inscription. Orientalia, 41(4), 457-468.

Quinn, J. (2018). In search of the Phoenicians. Princeton et al.: Princeton University Press.

Renfrew, C. (1987), Archaeology and language: the puzzle of Indo-European origins, London: Jonathan Cape.

Rohl, D. (2010). The Lords of Avaris. New York: Random House.

Sayce, A. H. (1911). Recent Biblical Archaeology. The Expository Times, 22(5), 226–229.

Schwabe, C., Adams, J., & Hodge, C. (1982). Egyptian Beliefs about the Bull's Spine: An Anatomical Origin for Ankh. Anthropological Linguistics, 24(4), 445-479. Retrieved March 26, 2021, from http://www.jstor.org/stable/30027646

Silius Italicus, T. C., & Duff, J. D. (1941). Punica. Cambridge, Mass.: London: Harvard University Press; William Heinemann.

Šprajc, I. (1993). The Venus-rain-maize complex in the Mesoamerican world view: part I. Journal for the History of Astronomy, 24(1-2), 17-70.

Strabo (1923). Geography, Volume II: Books 3-5. Translated by Horace Leonard Jones. Loeb Classical Library 50. Cambridge, MA: Harvard University Press.

Toscano, F. G. (2014). El Bronce Final en Huelva. Una visión preliminar del poblamiento en su ruedo agrícola a partir del registro arqueológico de La Orden-Seminario/Late Bronze Age at Huelva. A preliminary view of settlement patterns in its chora throught the study of the archaeological record of the Orden Seminario site. Complutum, 25(1), 139-158.

Trumbull, H. C. (1898). The Blood Covenant: A Primitive Rite, and Its Bearing on Scripture. 3rd Edition. Philadelphia: JD Wattles.

Tunisian women free to marry non-Muslims (September, June 15), BBC News. Retrieved from https://www.bbc.co.uk/news/world-africa-41278610

Van Dijk, R. (2013). Bull-leaping in the ancient Near East. Journal for Semitics, 22(1), 144-162.

Virgil. (1995). The Aeneid. Translated by Michael J. Oakley. Ware, Hertfordshire: Wordsworth Editions.

Waal, W. (2018). On the 'Phoenician Letters': The Case for an Early Transmission of the Greek Alphabet from an Archaeological, Epigraphic, and Linguistic Perspective. Aegean Studies, 1, 83-125.

Whiston, W. (1737). 'Flavius Josephus Against Apion', The genuine works of Flavius Josephus the Jewish historian. Cambridge: University of Cambridge Press.

Whitmarsh, T. (2016). Battling the Gods: Atheism in the Ancient World. London: Faber & Faber.

Wilkinson, R. H. (2003). The complete gods and goddesses of ancient Egypt. New York: Thames & Hudson.

Ziemann, M., & Seminar, C. (2015). 'The Drowned God: Are Melicertes and Melqart Identical?', Carthage Seminar, Ohio State University.

Chapter Seven

Celtiberian Merchant Empires

"When the German and Scythian nations overran the western provinces of the Roman empire...the violence which the barbarians exercised against the ancient inhabitants, interrupted the commerce between the towns and the country..."

Adam Smith, The Wealth of Nations (1872)

"Whoever for devotion alone...goes to Jerusalem to liberate the Church of God can substitute the journey for all penance".

Pope Urban II, Liber Lamberti (c.1095)

The Celtic Visigoths

In this chapter I will seek to discuss the Celtiberians in more detail, specifically in the context of the events that followed after the fall of Rome in 476 AD, prior to the conquest of the Americas in 1492 AD and in relation to a narrative of profitability and 'Parias' (tribute). Indeed, Visigothic Spain can be said to have continued to engage in the millennia old Tribute system defined by Carthage and continued by Rome until the Visigothic Kingdom of King Euric (466-484) and his capital at Toulouse was recognised as an independent territory by the Western Roman Emperor Julius Nepos (Mathisen, 2020: 407).

The Visigothic consolidation of territory in Iberia and the death of King Euric are considered to have contributed to the "customary Gothic cowardice...[and] that Frankish ability" (Mathisen, 2020: 408) to capture territories now part of modern France. Religion and Celtic Christianity play a big part in this historical narrative that led to the creation of France as well as Spain, as demonstrated by a famous quote attributed to the French leader Charles De Gaulle. He is thought to have said that "the history of France [began] with Clovis" (Gratton, 2012: 230). If he did indeed utter those words, it demonstrates that De Gaulle understood European sovereignty as a "secularised remnant of the authority of the medieval [Roman] church" (Gratton, 2012: 5) granted to Celtic tribal leaders after the fall of Rome.

Roman Christianity was officially introduced in 313 AD by the Emperor Constantine in the Edict of Milan as "the religion of the Empire" (Moore, 1942: 151). In medieval times the Christian God's church would continue to serve a as a legitimising force and be used to encourage hereditary power and the foundation of an Aristocracy across Europe. Therefore, despite the teachings of Jesus Christ about humility, sacrifice and equality forming the foundation of the Roman Catholic Church, its political influence meant that Roman Christianity was used as the legitimising force that underpinned the stability and sacrifice of Medieval serfdom through a chance at paradise via a "promised regeneration" (Moore, 1942: 151).

169

In the quotation at the beginning of this chapter Adam Smith states quite emphatically the importance of political stability, in his case, a 'Pax Romana', for commerce to flourish in a Roman Europe. He describes the period after the fall of Rome, that commonly has come to be known as the 'Dark Ages, negatively and as a regressive, unstable and fearful time in Europe. To Adam Smith, Visigothic Europe was a lawless place where life was considered by historians who utilise the same narrative as "nasty, brutish and short" (Hobbes, 1909: 97) without the Pax of a Roman Leviathan. However, the reality may have been somewhat different.

In the 'Dark Ages' the myriad of Celtic feudal settlements and fragmented successor states that had emerged in Iberia and tended to be localised, agricultural societies, as opposed to forming part of a much greater globalised system of trade like the Roman Empire or the Carthaginian Empire before it, were united under King Euric (466-484) and bound to the laws written by him in the Gallo-Romano Codex titled 'The Code of Euric'. According to Isidore of Seville (c.550 AD), in Iberia the Celtic Visigoths were the biggest of the organised groups and they had migrated southwards from Gaul. The second of these large migratory groups were the Germanic Suevi who had crossed the Danube to finally settle in Galicia.

In this historical context, King Euric of the Visigoths, King Clovis of the Franks and his descendent the Emperor Charlemagne may have only been mere mortals, but their contributions to the new political structures that emerged in Europe after the fall of the Roman Empire have continued to endure and inspire the federal structure of the European Union today. Economist Stanley Benn states that "the order of society…is only maintained because of certain rules or norms which are very variable, and which depend upon human desires and decision. This is not to say that all such rules have been consciously thought out and instituted; for what we call customs quite obviously have not" (Benn et al., 2013: 15).

Muslim Iberia

It can be argued that the Germanic Clans (Celtic: Klann) that dominated as the Franks in the Northern part of Western Europe and as the Visigoths of the Southern part of Western Europe emerged out of this period of political uncertainty through an understanding of metallurgy, political organisation and good planning at a time when plentiful resources depended on good harvests, fortifications and reliable weather. Education, a good work ethic and a fire for learning and technological advancement allowed Euric and Clovis to forge vast Kingdoms and a stable political structure which later generations built upon. However, in Iberia this Germanic vision would quickly lose momentum with the collapse of the Visigothic hold on Iberia under King Roderic following his defeat, death and the deaths of his top brass at the Battle of Guadalete (711 AD) that took place at a field east of Cadiz or 'Qadis' (Arabic: قادس) where a combination of exhaustion from fighting the Basques in the north and disloyalty from his own nobles who sought to challenge his reign from within his own camp, opened the door to the Muslim conquest of Iberia. At first, the Muslims would take over the Visigothic territory of 'Hispania Baetis' and rename it Al-Andalus (Arabic: الأَنْدَلُس)(Spanish: Andalucía). They would then expand northwards past the Baetis river which the Muslims renamed the 'al-Wadi 'l-Kabir' (Arabic: الْكَبِيرْ الْوَادِي) commonly spelt as the 'Guadalquivir' which means 'the great valleys' in Arabic. What was left of the Visigoths retreated to the mountainous terrain of Northern Iberia.

Following the Muslim conquest of a great part of the Iberian Peninsula after the Battle of Guadalete, Historian Lionel Jane surmises that the Visigoths by being driven north may have been imbued with the "very physical characteristics of... the [northern point of the Iberian] peninsula, and ...the physical characteristic of Castile" (Jane, 1966: 19). As such, Jane's assumption is that the mediaeval leaders of the Celtiberian civilizations that found themselves pinned in northern Iberia may have grown accustomed to a siloed mentality and used their hierarchies to create clans, each with its own micro-nation from the east coast to west coast across the northern part of the Iberian Peninsula that valued their "individual liberty and local freedom" (Jane, 1966: 19) above all, and for centuries nurtured an impatience for authority, a need for self-reliance and an obstinate dependence on their own efforts that is still part of Hispanic culture to this day.

Historian Lionel Jane's Gothic centred narrative can serve to suggest that after the Muslim invasion in Northern Iberia every Celtic Kingdom that remained in Iberia became, if not an island, then at least a remote castle fortified by the defensive geography of the "rugged mountain ranges" (Jane, 1966: 19) in the Northern territories of Spain. Indeed, these Kingdoms of Spain in their nascent state as the Visigothic Kingdom of Asturias and Basque Kingdom of Navarre, would shape the foundation upon which a host of castles would be built on, especially once those Celtic peoples arrived in Venezuela. The Kingdom of Navarre and the later incarnations of the 'Basque Country' (Spanish: País Vasco) was the ancestral home of Venezuela's most celebrated leader, Simon Bolivar (1783-1830).

Moreover, exile to the northern fringes of the Iberian territory may have meant that the recklessness, petty rivalries, aggression and desire for independence bred out by war or King's displeasure in the gentlemen and aristocracies of other European countries, were preserved unscathed in Asturias and Navarre protected by their mountainous terrain, for at least seven-hundred years prior to Columbus' Atlantic voyage in 1492 and subsequently exported 'sold as seen' to the New World. From this exile and rugged geography, we slowly see emerge the Medieval Kingdoms of Asturias, Galicia, Leon, Castile, Navarre, Aragon and Portugal. Kingdoms born out of the rocky northern Iberian Celtic territory of Asturias that remained a territorial outlier on the peninsula during the Muslim conquest of Spain and the subsequent establishment of the Muslim 'Califate of Cordoba' (Arabic: خلافة قرطبة).

The nature of this Spanish exodus to the north is made all the more palpable by the archaeological evidence from Madrid which shows that during the 8th Century, around the year 750, there was "general and sudden desertion" (Castillo, 2006: 110) of villages south of the river Duero. In fact, "none of the villages founded in

Madrid in the early medieval period appear to have survived into the Middle Ages with their original form location" (Castillo, 2006: 110). Moreover, as recent as 2003, archaeological evidence from Galicia in northwest Spain has shown that the terraced farming plots at the valley of Oitavén that are "still in use today" (Ballesteros-Arias, 2003: 28) date to the reign of Pelagius of Asturias (c. 685 – 737), its first King.

Indeed, not only does this evidence demonstrate the enduring quality of the agrarian structures created during the Visigothic period that attempted to make the most out of the hilly terrain of Galicia, but also the Asturian's ability to follow a precise plan based on the "collective work of a whole community" (Castillo, 2006: 112). Furthermore, in Medieval Europe "eighty to 90 percent of the population...was engaged in arable and pastoral farming" (Seccombe, 1992: 78) and the communities of Northern Spain were no different. The corporate foundation of Feudal Europe was the lord's manor, which was run as a 'demesne' (home farm) worked by servants (Celtic: amaeth) and could include the use of plots leased to tenant farmers or vassals (Celtic: wassalo).

In Northern Spain, compared to the rest of Europe, for the rich (Celtic: rīg) Lords of the manor "there was no certain hope of any adequate reward for labour" (Jane, 1966: 20) and it seemed that nature urged them "to prey upon their fellows" (Jane, 1966: 20), "to care each for himself alone, to refuse submission to others" (Jane, 1966: 20) while ironically, expecting others to submit, and "...to care nothing for peace or good order" (Jane, 1966: 20).

Given the above historical and archaeological context to build an account of the nature of these Gothic Spaniards that first set foot in Venezuela, we can begin to understand the frustration felt by Simon Bolivar(1783-1830), a son of Navarre venerated as the Liberator of South America, some three-hundred years later, towards a proudly self-reliant people whom he sought to control, would cause him to lament that "[Latin] America is ungovernable; those who served the revolution have ploughed the sea" (Liss, 1972: 133).

Also, we begin to find empirical and a historical context for Spanish colloquial phrases like 'no hay moros en la costa' (the coast is clear), literally meaning 'there are no Moors on the coast', a linguistic throwback to this isolated, paranoid and uncertain period where the Spanish Kingdoms in the North "averse from any form of union, mutually suspicious or mutually hostile" (Jane, 1966: 19), were constantly scanning the coast for ships of al-Andalusian origin, as well as watching their own backs.

The fact that "communication was never easy and was often practically impossible" (Jane, 1966: 19) over such rugged terrain may have meant an increased isolation between the various political factions controlling northern Spain. Moreover, the expression 'Como Pedro por su casa' or 'Como Pedro por Huesca' (he does what he wants) an idiom of early medieval origin that came about from Peter I of Aragon and Navarre's military victory at the Battle of Alcoraz (1096) outside of Huesca, against the Independent Muslim principality or 'Taifas' (Arabic: طائفة) of Zaragoza, is another throwback expression to the Reconquista,

175

although one similar in tone to the football chant 'he does what he wants', which can either be a pejorative or flattering comment towards the intended target.

Nevertheless, from this Celtic historical perspective, no linguistic artefact from this period has had the same influence or effect on the modern-day Spanish and Venezuelan imagination as the legend of 'El Cid' (Arabic: سيد) which translates as 'The Mister', also known as 'the Centaur' (Arabic: القنبيطور), a brave adventurer, strategist and captain of a private army, all rolled into one. The link between ruggedness, isolationist, aggressive and romantic notions of Spanish chivalry would be defined and codified during the years of the Reconquista (711-1492), especially through the stories told about 'El Cid' Rodrigo Diaz de Vivar, commonly referred to as 'El Campeador' (The Champion), a clever rogue and mercenary who would become a living legend and the Spanish herculean hero worthy of many an equestrian statue.

In church propaganda, 'El Cid' was painted as a Christian warrior who brought war successfully to the Muslims of Southern Spain, especially King Ahmed of Valencia in 1094. However, 'El Cid' "was as ready to fight alongside Muslims against Christians as vice versa" (Fletcher, 1991: 4), depending on who his paymaster was. Nevertheless, the enduring quality of this early medieval Spanish hero has been that his legend was useful to demonstrate that Spanish "territory was regained by those who relied upon themselves" (Jane, 1966: 20). Celtic Christian propaganda propagated by Castilian heroic poetry about 'El Cid' (Penny, 2002:

15) would serve to demonstrate Celtic superiority over their Islamic rivals.

Figure 33: Equestrian Statues: 1. El Cid, 2. Simón Bolívar, 3. Simón Bolívar

Indeed, this narrative of self-reliance at the core of Spanish sensibilities, can even be observed in recent Venezuelan history, through the actions of brave individuals like Venezuelan policeman Oscar Alberto Perez, who stood up to the machinations of Nicolas Maduro's dictatorship and paid for it with his life in 2018 and the actions of a humble gang leader called Wilexis from the Caracas favela of Petare, who stood up against the poverty and hunger associated with the economic mismanagement of Maduro's dictatorship and also paid for it with his life. Like 'El Cid', these men built around them a private army, but neither had the necessary assistance or luck to triumph against the overwhelming odds of Maduro's own private 'Bolivarian' forces.

Figure 34: A Poster of Oscar Perez c.2020

Figure 35: A Poster of Leopoldo Lopez c.2013

In contrast, while mixed race Venezuelans like Wilexis and Oscar Perez paid for their political uprisings with their lives, the opposition leader Leopoldo Lopez faced a prison sentence and house arrest which he was able to escape to the safety of a Spanish Embassy in Caracas that granted him refuge. It must be noted that the Spanish descended political elites in Venezuela have historically intermarried with the families of other political elites and therefore their bloodlines show little evidence of the same characteristics as the native and mixed populations of Venezuela.

The 'Parias Formula'

Moreover, it can be said that the Castilian habit to seek 'parias' (English: tribute) of its own, mentioned earlier in the book, found encouragement during the reign of Fernando I of Castile when he successfully subdued from 1050 to 1060 the Kingdoms of Pamplona (Navarre), Zaragoza and León and began to launch raids against most of the Independent Muslim Taifas of the south forcing them all to pay 'parias' "providing Fernando, the means to wage war against [them]" (Catlos, 2018: 223).

Pope Urban II quoted at the beginning of this chapter who unleashed the First crusade upon Jerusalem in 1095 by giving a convincing sermon at the Council of Clermont, would also play his part to encourage Fernando I of Castile's aggressive stance against the Taifas of al-Andalus by supporting his claims over the whole of the Iberian Peninsula. Indeed, the Kingdom of León-Castile was also granted exclusive rights in battle to the use of imagery designed for the radical and bloodthirsty cult of St. James 'Matamoros' (English: Moor vanquisher), with its epicentre at the Santiago de Compostela Cathedral, the last stop of the pilgrimage

179

that still takes place on the ancient Roman road that connected Burdigala (Bordeaux) in Aquitaine with Brigantia (La Coruña) in Gallaecia (Orosius, 1.2) and was renamed the St. James Way.

In fact, many of the wars in the Iberian Peninsula during the Reconquista of Spain were "consecrated crusades by the Papacy" (Catlos, 2018: 4), including some of which were fought against other Christian Kingdoms of Iberian Peninsula. Indeed, in a land "fractured by rivalries and crisscrossed by alliances that bore little relation to religious identity" (Catlos, 2018: 335), for centuries raiding became such a way of life that Historian Brian Catlos characterises the Spanish Kingdoms as societies that became "organised for war" (Catlos, 2018: 4). These Celtic descended Spanish Kingdoms would even turn on the Celts of the Occitan during the Albigensian crusade (1209-1229) when the Cathars were deemed infidels worthy of complete destruction by Rome.

During this time of increasingly sanctioned Christian bloodshed, the battle of Las Navas de Tolosa (1212) would herald a change of leadership in Islamic southern Spain. The defeat would signal weakness in the Almohad forces who still controlled half of the territory on the Iberian Peninsula. This victory, at the time, was interpreted by Rodrigo Jimenez de Rada the Archbishop of Toledo from 1209-1247 as a "divine triumph and a vindication of [a] Castilian manifest destiny" (Catlos, 2018: 283) against the Almohad Califate of King al-Nasir, and would not have been won without the fighting troops that had been drawn to fight in the battle by the Crusade Bull from Pope Innocent III that inspired Christians to commit atrocities in the name of their religion.

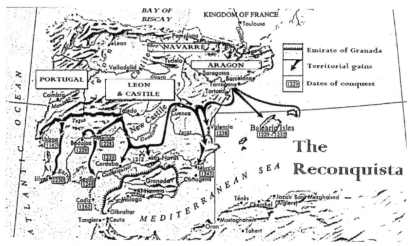

Figure 36: A Map of the 3rd Stage of The Reconquista

Indeed, the army that Alfonso VIII would muster to fight King al-Nasir would be composed of troops from most of the Christian Kingdoms of Spain, apart from the Kingdom of Leon. Nevertheless, this was not a united Spain, but rather a host of common interests coming together to form the Castilian-led forces of Alfonso VIII. When the Castilian King had defeated al-Nasir at 'Las Navas' and plundered his treasure left abandoned in his tent when he fled the battle, his coalition subsequently disbanded to the frustration of Catholic scholars like the aforementioned Archbishop of Toledo. Alfonso would not capitalise on his victory to change the map of Spain, but other Monarchs would use his momentum to continue their onslaught on the Islamic Taifas.

It must be noted that the Kingdom of Navarre, the modern-day Basque Country, denied by geographical location from making territorial gains during the conquest of Islamic Spain, would initially focus on its rivalry with the Kingdom of Castile and under the leadership of French Aristocrat Theobald IV of Champagne (1229) would answer the call of Pope Gregory IX to join the Barons' crusade (1239) and send Navarre's resources towards Jerusalem and the Middle East. For King Theobald the Middle East and Constantinople would offer him access to spices, silks and other luxury goods that could be traded in Spain and across Europe.

Theses riches are discussed in the travels of Marco Polo published as 'Il Milione' (English: The Million), said to be short for 'The Million Lies', published around 1295 but can be used to relate the sheer size, importance and wealth Europeans would also come to associate with the Silk Road at this time and might have even served to inspire an ambitious Genoese citizen by the name of Christopher Columbus two hundred years later. Moreover, with the fall of Constantinople in 1453 and Ottoman Empire's control over the Eastern Mediterranean, spices, silks and other luxury goods, "were marked up tenfold" (Koning et al., 1992: 13) to European merchants. This meant that "the Enterprise of the Indies" (Koning et al., 1992: 13) became an interesting and lucrative proposition.

Prince Henry the Navigator of Portugal was the trail blazer who sought shipping routes around the horn of Africa. In 1486, Bartolomeu Diaz would round the Cape of Good Hope and in 1498, after a 9-month voyage Vasco da Gama would finally reach the shores of India. With an established trade route, it stands to reason why it was the Spanish crown rather than Portugal who ultimately accepted and funded Christopher Columbus' radical proposal of charting a new route to Asia by sailing west. It must be noted that that it is speculated that in 1489 Bartholomew Columbus (the brother of Christopher Colombus) also approached Henry VII with his Grand Enterprise and he "turned him down flat" (Davidson, 1997: 43). However, there is no conclusive proof to support this speculation.

Figure 37: J.B. Bury, Map of the Spanish Kingdoms 1360 During the Castilian Civil War (1351-1369)

Moreover, conquest over the 'Taifa' territories did not just bring new lands under the control of the Spanish Kingdoms but also access to as host of new information. The surrender of Toledo in 1085 did not only grant the Visigoths their lost capital city but also the intellectual riches of the Great Library at Toledo. The 'Siete

183

Partidas' (English: The Seven Part Code) penned by Alphonse X (1221 –1284) the King of Castile, Leon and Galicia, may be said to have been a result of this Reconquista Renaissance and growing Spanish influence. Alphonse X's Codex, which is viewed in the Spanish speaking world as their equivalent of the English Magna Carta, was not actually the first of its kind, since the 'Code of Euric' (c. 480 AD) and 'Lex Visigothorum' of King Chindasuinth (642–653 AD) had marked an earlier transition from Roman Law to the Germanic Law of the ruling Visigoths.

Figure 38: Las Siete Partidas reprinted 1611 (under King Phillip III)

Finally, with the conquest of the Emirate of Granada in 1492 may have come the architectural inspiration from the Cordoba Mosque and its Moorish arches and Moorish windows that would in turn go on to inspire the Colonial style of architecture that is still a big part of Venezuela's cultural history and national identity and examples can be seen throughout Venezuela and Latin America.

Not to mention the use of 'Spanish gardens' in the design of public buildings like the Capitol building in Caracas, a design inspired by the walled paradise or 'faradis' (Arabic: سيدارَة) gardens of Andalucía, that in turn could trace back its design to the first civilization in Mesopotamia and the gardens at Edin.

Klein-Venedig

The victory at Granada would also be the reason why Pedro Margarit, a long-term dependent of the crown, would be honoured in the Royal decree of June 7, 1491, for his "great and noble service in this war of Granada" (Davidson, 1997: 362). Following the discovery of the Americas, the Bishop Bartolomé de las Casas would write that under Pedro Margarit's leadership and command the Spaniards in the Americas stole the native's "food, women and daughters" (Davidson, 1997: 363).

When it comes to the territory that has now come to be known as Venezuela or 'Klein-Venedig' in the original High German, we can either focus entirely on the historical negatives and atrocities, ponder over what might have been had Columbus' ships sunk during their Atlantic crossing in 1492, or instead, assess the devastation caused by a five-hundred-year-old military invasion and its latest chapter of human tragedy. Miles H. Davidson notes that "strangest of all" (Davidson, 1997: 358) Columbus sent his Chief Accountant Bernal Diaz de Pisa (1494) to monitor the transactions between his men and the indigenous communities they traded foodstuffs with because Colombus found his men to be greedy, which angered the natives. This was followed by a decree by Queen Isabella of Castille declaring the indigenous peoples to be "free vassals of the crown" (Altman, 2003: 143).

By 1503, a Royal decree was issued establishing the 'Casa de Contratación de las Indias' (English: The House of Trade of the Indies) in the port of Seville with Rodríguez de Fonseca as the de facto "Minister of the Colonies" (Serrera, 2008: 133). In 1509 Alonso de Ojeda with the permission of the Spanish crown led an expedition to the Venezuelan coast as part of the 'Andalusian Journeys'. During his exploration of the Paraguaná Peninsula in modern North-Western Venezuela his fleet discovered the 'Gulf of Venezuela' and sailed into it to discover Lake Maracaibo where they first encountered the Wayuu people living on wooden stilt houses the natives called 'palafitos' built along the shore of Lake Maracaibo.

In its earliest written history, the polity of Venezuela was referred to as Klein-Venedig (En. *Little Venice*) by its German Governor Nikolaus Federmann in his book *Indianische Historia* (Indian History) published in 1557, presumably a name inspired by the wooden stilt houses of the Wayuu. The territory Alonso de Ojeda discovered was a domain that was granted to the Welser family of Augsburg in 1528 by the Holy Roman Emperor Charles V (Charles I of Spain). This move is seen by some historians as an effort to settle the substantial debts the monarch had built up with the Welser Bank, an accounting practice observed at the time as "counting unpaid loan balances as fictive advances in a new contract" (Tracy, 2002: 309) and by other historians as simply the traditional practices of Spanish Kings to their vassals (Friede, 1961: 135).

However, in this regard the latter suggestion appears out of context. It must be noted that by 1529 Emperor Charles V had also "pawned his interests in the Moluccas [Islands]" (Tracy, 2002: 308) in the Asian Pacific, more commonly known as the Spice Islands, in exchange for Portuguese gold. Moreover, Charles I's electoral campaign to be crowned Holy Roman Emperor by the Pope in 1530 would have been partly funded by the Welsers and the Fuggers of Augsburg, who sought to "persuade the empire's seven electoral princes to vote for the right candidate" (Tracy, 2002: 99).

This electoral 'donation' was documented as being 851,918 Rhine Gulden, equivalent to about 602,026 ducats, roughly $112,500,000 based on today's gold exchange rate, and would not be the last Gulden Emperor Charles V would need from his banker allies. In fact, he would continue to rely on the Banking families of Welser, Fugger and Grimaldi throughout his reign to secure loans that he would then use to finance his many costly wars overseas (Tracy, 2002: 308). This self-styled new Charlemagne and universal monarch would also adopt the Pillars of Hercules and the Latin motto 'Plus Ultra' (English: Further beyond) onto his Coat of Arms, clearly the Latin equivalent of Star Trek's "to boldly go where no man has gone before" (Roddenberry 1966) , the motto being an "inversion of the note said by Le Fèvre to have been pinned to one of [the pillars] by Hercules" (Bull 2009: 163) to assert "a determination to go 'further still'" (Bull 2009: 163), a phrase still present in modern popular culture and a central tenant of Friedrich Nietzsche's philosophy of the Übermensch.

Figure 39: J.B. Modern Flag of Spain. The current design of the King of Spain's Coat of Arms
was created in 1981 but retains the Pillars of Hercules and the motto Plus Ultra
(Further Beyond).

This Feudal political narrative and toxic masculinity combined with the active Christianisation of the Americas during the early modern period meant the inevitable genetic Europeanisation of the native Amerindians. Indeed, historical evidence points to a law passed in 1514 that legitimised marriage between the indigenous peoples and the Spanish colonists and genetic evidence has found conclusive proof that "when the Europeans arrived in the Caribbean they readily mated with Amerindian females" (Madrigal, 2006: 121), which is why DNA studies on modern day Venezuelans show that 90% of Venezuelans have a European genetic component (mostly from Spain) which ranges from 40-60%, an Amerindian component which ranges from 20-35% and an African component of 10-20%. It should be noted that the Amerindian component is more likely to be passed down from a female rather than male Amerindian ancestor (Madrigal, 2006: 139-140).

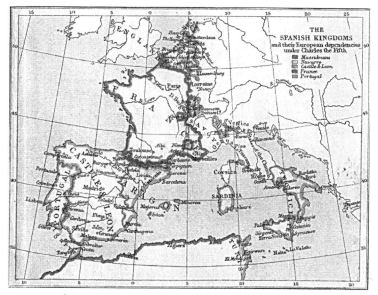

Figure 40: J.B. Bury, Map of the Spanish Kingdoms and their European Dependencies under Hapsburg Emperor Charles V

In the meantime, while this 'Westworld' was taking off in Latin America, the ruling "Hapsburgs in Spain had become more Spanish than the Spaniards" (Jane, 1966: 83). The Holy Roman Emperor Charles V squarely "identified himself with the nation of his mother" (Jane, 1966: 83) Juana the Mad (1479 –1555) and became the proto-typical Castilian male. Moreover, although his grandfather Ferdinand II of Aragon had "turned to Jewish bankers to finance the conquest of Granada (1492)" (Tracy, 2002: 94) as Jewish firms lost their favour and prominence amidst the growing anti-Semitism in Spain and the creation of the royal tribunal the Spanish Inquisition (1492) under queen Isabella of Castile, it was the German banking families based in Augsburg that took their place.

Indeed, by 1519 as Charles V gained trading privileges overseas and Hapsburg interests turned westward, the Fugger and Welser Banking corporations of Augsburg moved from "lending against the Hapsburg Dynasty's Austrian mining rights to lending against its Castilian and Neapolitan revenues" (Tracy, 2002: 99) and in 1521-1523, the Grimaldi and Centurione families had gained the "contract for administering the lands of three military orders that had been annexed to the crown" (Tracy, 2002: 94). Nevertheless, it was in Zaragoza, Spain 1528, thirty-six years after Christopher Columbus had made his first journey to the Americas that Emperor Charles V granted the Welsers, specifically their agents in Zaragoza Heinrich Ehinger, an aristocrat from the city of Constance in modern day Germany, and Hieronymus Sailer, who would later marry Felicitas Welser the daughter of the head of the Welser family, Bartholomew Welser, the rights to Klein-Venedig to "smooth...pacify the land and populate it" and "place it in [Charles'] service in a manner that [the King] can profit from it" (Montenegro, 2018: 24).

Moreover, the Welsers were contractually bound to create two cities and establish a colony in Klein-Venedig (Venezuela). To achieve their aims Sailer and Ehinger acquired licenses to ship 4,000 African slaves to America, recruited 300 colonists and equipped four ships for their first expedition to Venezuela. In 1524-30, several larger pension and loan transactions were also occupied with the Spanish crown this financial risk taken partly in cooperation with the Fugger company. By 1530, Sailer and Ehinger having failed to colonise Klein-Venedig officially transferred the rights to Venezuela to the brothers Bartholomäus Welser and Anton Welser who hired Ambrosio Dalfinger to represent their interests as Governor of the Province.

In those days, the fable of an 'El Dorado' (English: The Golden One) in Latin America was at the forefront in the mind of every colonist who set foot on Venezuelan soil. The Welsers believed that finding 'El Dorado' would mean recovering their investment and rumour had it that it was located near the Xuruara territory inhabited by the Caiquetio tribe. This rumour is believed to have spread by the Coquivacoa tribe and their Chieftain Maracaibo. Klein-Vendig's German Governor Nikolaus Federmann, from his settlement at Coro in the Paraguana Peninsula would lead an expedition through the First Nations of Venezuela (Montenegro, 2018: 25). To get to El Dorado, Ambrosio Dalfinger would travel south through Caiquetio territory from the Paraguana peninsula and through modern-day Falcón state, then west through the Xuruara territory and south again into Yukpa territory once he reached the Maracaibo basin and the territory of the Wayuu.

In his memoir 'Indianische Historia' (Indian History) published in 1557, Nikolaus Federmann tells of the expedition he led into the interior of Klein-Venedig in 1530–31. In his account of the events, he details what he encountered when he first landed in the port of Coro. The absent Governor Ambrosio Dalfinger who had gone on expedition was presumed held captive by the natives or dead (Federmann, 1916: 23) by the Welsers. In Dalfinger's absence

Hans Seissenhoffer had been named the Governor of the province and on arrival Nikolaus Federmann took on the duties as Seissenhoffer's Lieutenant. Fifteen days after Federmann's arrival at Coro the missing Governor Ambrosio Dalfinger was spotted travelling towards the port of Coro after an eight-month long absence. Upon hearing the news, Seissenhoffer resigned from his position as Governor of the Province.

Figure 41: Willem Jansz. Blaeu's Map of Venezuela circa 1640, Amsterdam

While exploring the interior of his Province Dalfinger had lost about one hundred men to "combat and diseases" (Federmann, 1916: 24). The expedition had taken a physical toll on him, and shortly after retuning Dalfinger resigned as Governor and retuned to the island of Santo Domingo, leaving Nikolaus Federmann as highest-ranking officer, in charge of the Province of Klein-Venedig.

Left at a loose end, Federmann decided to venture inland with a 110 Spanish infantrymen, 16 horsemen and accompanied by 100 indigenous Caquetíos who served as their luggage handlers (Federmann, 1916: 28) to explore the uncharted terrain. What followed was the complete disaster that one might expect when wandering into hostile terrain.

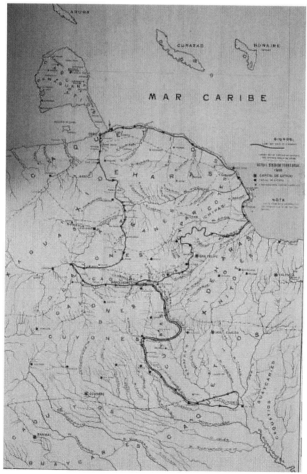

Figure 42: Federman's Expedition 1530-31 (Federman, 1916: 8)

Suffice to say, their ambitions ended in failure and the frustration caused by these failures to manage Klein-Venedig ultimately meant that the Welser concession was revoked by Charles V in 1546. This insatiable drive towards materialism and commodities would be the driving force of the early story of Caracas, founded by the Spanish explorer Francisco Fajardo in 1558. This driving force behind the human-led catastrophe that befell Venezuela and the Americas, which nearly wiped out the native inhabitants of the First Nations of Venezuela and installed the series of disastrous non-native regimes doing their best to profit from the land and their misappropriated gains, especially in the wider Amazon, Orinoco and Maracaibo basins, will be explored further in the next volume, 'The Rake's Progress' in a historical narrative that will seek to culminate in the present day failed sate of Venezuela where the Communism of Nicolas Maduro's de facto regime continues to grip onto power.

Bibliography

Altman, I., Cline, S. L., & Pescador, J. J. (2003). The Early History of Greater Mexico. Upper Saddle River, N.J.: Prentice Hall.

Ballesteros-Arias, P. (2003). La arqueología en la gasificación de Galicia 17: El paisaje agrario. Universidad de Santiago de Compostela, p.28

Bartolomé, de Las Casas, Historia de las Indias (ed. Juan, Pérez de Tudela Bueso), Biblioteca de Autores Españoles, Vols. XCV—XCVI (Madrid 1957), 1, 244, 263

Bird, J., Peters, E., & Powell, J. M. (Eds.). (2013). Crusade and Christendom: Annotated Documents in Translation from Innocent III to the Fall of Acre, 1187-1291. Pennsylvania: University of Pennsylvania Press.

Bull, M. (2006). The mirror of the gods: Classical mythology in Renaissance art. London: Penguin Books.

Castillo, J. A. Q., & Guirado, A. V. E. (2006). Networks of peasant villages between Toledo and Uelegia Alabense, Northwestern Spain (V–Xth centuries). Archeologia medievale, Vol. 33, All'Insegna del Giglio, pp.79-128.

Catlos, B. A. (2018). Kingdoms of Faith: A New History of Islamic Spain. Oxford: Oxford University Press.

Davidson, M. H. (1997). Columbus then and now: a life re-examined. Norman, Oklahoma: University of Oklahoma Press.

Diaz, R., 2012. The Amazon of Matinino: A Personal Legacy of Female Empowerment in the Greater Antilles. Journal of the Motherhood Initiative for Research and Community Involvement, 3(2).

Federmann, N. (1916). Narración del primer viaje de Federmann a Venezuela, Translated by Arcaya, Pedro Manuel, 1874-1958, Caracas: Lit. y Tip. del Comercio.

Fletcher, R. A. (1991). The Quest for El Cid. Oxford: Oxford University Press.

Friede, J. (1961). Los Welser En La Conquista De Venezuela. Caracas: Ediciones Edime.

Hermans, R. A. (2017). Latin cults through Roman eyes: Myth, memory and cult practice in the Alban hills. Doctoral dissertation, Universiteit van Amsterdam.

Jane, C. (1966). Liberty and Despotism in Spanish America. Preface by Salvador de Madariaga. New York: Cooper Square Publishers.

Koning, H., & Bigelow, B. (1992). Columbus: His enterprise: Exploding the myth. New York: Monthly Review Press.

Levene, R. (1973). Las Indias no eran colonias. Buenos Aires et al.: Espasa-Calpe Argentina.

Madrigal, L. (2006). Human biology of Afro-Caribbean populations (Vol. 45). Cambridge: Cambridge University Press.

Montenegro, G. (2018) "The Welser Phantom": Apparitions of the Welser Venezuela Colony in Nineteenth and Twentieth-Century German Cultural Memory, TRANSIT, vol. 11, no. 2.

Nietzsche, F. (1896) Thus Spake Zarathustra, translated by Alexander Tille. New York: Macmillan Press.

Orosius, P. (2010). Seven books of history against the pagans (Vol. 54). Liverpool: Liverpool University Press.

Penny, R. J. (2002). A history of the Spanish language. Cambridge: Cambridge University Press.

Pidal, R. M. (2016). The Cid and His Spain. New York: Routledge.

Redon, A. (2017). Female warriors of the Viking age. Final paper in Master-degree in Archaeology, University of Iceland.

Roddenberry, G. (1966) "Gene Roddenberry Star Trek Television Series Collection". UCLA Library. https://www.library.ucla.edu/blog/special/2016/10/11/to-boldly-go-the-hurried-evolution-of-star-treks-opening-narration

Roscher, W. H. (Ed.). (1894). Ausführliches Lexikon der griechischen und römischen Mythologie: Bd., 1. Abt. Iache-Kyzikos. 1890-1894 (Vol. 2). Leipzig : BG Teubner.

Serrera Contreras, R. M (2008). 'La Casa de la Contratación en el Alcázar de Sevilla (1503-1717)'. Boletín de la Real Academia Sevillana de Buenas Letras. 36: 141-176. Consultado el 24 de julio de 2014

Seccombe, W. (1992). A millennium of family change: feudalism to capitalism in North-western Europe. London; New York: Verso

Smith, A. (1872). On the Wealth of Nations. London : Alex Murray & Son.

Somerville, R. (1972). The Councils of Urban II. Vol. 1: Decreta Claromontensia. Amsterdam: Hakkert.

Starkie, W. (1957). The road to Santiago: Pilgrims of St. James. New York: E.P. Dutton.

Tracy, J. (1993) The Rise of Merchant Empires: Long Distance Trade in the Early Modern World, 1350-1750. Cambridge: Cambridge University Press.

Tracy, J. D. (2002). Emperor Charles V, impresario of war: campaign strategy, international finance, and domestic politics. Cambridge: Cambridge University Press.

Tremlett, G. (2017). Isabella of Castile: Europe's First Great Queen. London: Bloomsbury Publishing.

Whitehead, N.L. (1984). Carib cannibalism: The historical evidence. Journal de la Société des Américanistes, pp.69-87.

Epilogue

Introducing the Rake's Progress

"What a monument of human smallness is this idea of the philosopher king. What a contrast between it and the simplicity of humanness of Socrates, who warned the statesmen against the danger of being dazzled by his own power, excellence, and wisdom, and who tried to teach him what matters most – that we are all frail human beings..."

Karl Popper, The Open Society and Its Enemies

At the start of this book, we asked you to picture a real-life Westworld, a beautiful, lush land, rich in natural resources and peopled with thinking, feeling humans. As in Westworld, the adventurers who arrived were encouraged to enjoy and exploit this 'new' world, whether they were there to settle or merely plunder. As for the original inhabitants, the indigenous tribes, the Europeans behaved towards them as the humans behaved towards the Hosts in Westworld, killing, raping or stealing from them. Some of these acts of aggression may have been frowned upon by members of the clergy but overall, these acts were not treated as a crimes.

It is unsurprising, therefore, that this real life Westworld, where settlers, adventurers and native cultures were forcibly mixed together over the following five hundred years would form a

199

nation where violence, greed, exploitation and lust would become the pillars of that society. Therefore, one could argue that the current turmoil, is merely the latest act of a tragedy that will be called in its final volume 'Paradise Lost'.

As a Venezuelan historian and social scientist of International Affairs the author of this book saw that there was an unexplored rich tapestry to Venezuela's 500-year-old history that he wanted to share with you. Indeed, for those Venezuelans like the author who grew up abroad after the rise of Chavez's autocratic regime, Venezuela's history may seem messy, incomplete or told to us by those with vested political interests or through half-remembered quotes. Over the course of this first book, we have attempted to begin to unravel, analyse and explain the woven threads that have contributed to the development of the Venezuelan identity and discovered that the roots of that culture go deep into the earliest civilizations. However, we have only begun to explore this rich and complex tapestry.

In chapter one we introduced the question 'to what extent do cultural institutions influence the morphological changes in the long-term development of a culture' and throughout the book we have discovered that over millennia cultural institutions, such as myths, religion, family, culture, political hierarchies and language have had a profound contribution on the development of kinship, technology and diplomatic ties that led to the development of symbols, laws and the social structure of the people who would later be mixed together to form the various regional variations of Venezuelan identity.

In chapter two, 'The Maize of the Taino', this argument is expanded upon with a short study of the indigenous cultures that Christopher Columbus encountered in his first voyages to the Americas. We attempted to explore the ancient native American cultures that developed the horticultural skills that led to the development of many food staples that we take for granted in the west today like maize, sweet potatoes and tomatoes. A myriad of technological advancements that have saved countless generations across the globe from famine. Indeed, it is plausible to surmise that had the First Nations of Venezuela not been subjected to a full-scale military invasion, they would have certainly continued to thrive on the Venezuelan mainland and throughout the Caribbean.

In chapter three, 'Our Phoenician Alphabet', we began by discussing Venezuela as the 'Land of do as you please' in the context of myth creation and moral fables. We discussed the 5000-year-old remains of 'Calpeia' found on Gibraltar and the evidence left behind by the Neolithic Iberians, prior to the arrival of the Phoenicians to Iberian shores to seek to unravel the first principles that underlie Venezuela as the 'Land of do as you please'. DNA evidence coupled with the Upper Palaeolithic cave paintings found at the Cave of Altamira in Northern Spain dated at circa 35,000 BCE served to demonstrate how at the same time as the ancestors of the native Americans were making their way across the Bering strait, Neolithic Iberians were sheltering in caves and depicting their hunter gatherer lifestyle.

Arguably, an act of colonisation in Iberia took place by Phoenician colonists around who settled southern Iberia, created a colony in 'Cadiz' or 'Gadir' (Punic: 𐤂𐤃𐤓𐤀) around 1100 BCE (Quinn, 2018: 116) and drove the Neolithic Iberians northwards. In chapter four, 'The Fertile Crescent' we explored the development of the culture of these first colonists of Iberia the Phoenicians. We discussed the peoples of the Levant in the context of the ancient Mesopotamian civilization at Sumer and the myths of Eden and a religious practices that sprung up from that civilization and were subsequently depicted in the book of Genesis.

To unravel the story of the Canaanites who have become a central and misunderstood part of Hispanic Christian tradition, in chapter five, 'A Story Written in Egypt' we explored the ancient history of the Hyksos people of the Levant who settled and are believed to have controlled northern Egypt during the era of the 15th dynasty circa 1630–1523 BCE. In this context we explored the Biblical story in the Book of Exodus and attempted to convey the idea of a 'wheel of fortune' as a very real part of the ups and downs of human history.

In chapter six, 'From Carthage with Love', we return to north Africa to discuss the rise and fall of the Carthaginian civilization. The rise of Carthage has been interwoven with the myth of Queen Elissa and the Carthaginian goddess Tanit. Theses ancient myths and beliefs still positively influence modern-day Tunisia and are woven into the fabric of an increasingly egalitarian Tunisian democratic state.

In chapter seven, 'Celtiberian Merchant Empires' we explored the Celts and their rise to prominence after the fall of the Roman Empire. We contrast the Celts withy the previously discussed north African influence in the development of the bull fighting and jennet culture of Andalucía. Despite the destruction of Carthage, it became clear that what began with Phoenician colonists was cemented by Carthaginian ambitions and treasured by the post-Roman Visigoths who rose from the Kingdom of Asturias.

This first attempt at a comprehensive history of Venezuela is not even close to completion at the end of the first volume and the second volume 'A Rake's Progress' will begin by telling the tale of the African diaspora as Europeans gained a foothold in the Americas and prominence around the world, they required labour to 'colonise', in the old sense of the world to cultivate, the new world. The irony is that this process was driven by Celtic lineages that had themselves suffered under the yoke of an Imperial Roman power. However, it is clear that their adoption and understanding of its history was focused on a continuation of the Roman power structures that had come before them, rather than a move away from them. Therefore, by the time we get to Holy Roman Emperor Charles V, these political institutions can be seen to have foregone their Celtic past to become part of a new Roman myth. This confusion of ideas and culture was in the end exported into the heart to the Americas and Venezuela.

In conclusion, as we have reviewed over the course of this study, the history of Iberia over the last few millennia and the history of Venezuela over the past 500 years has been a story of the longest occupations in human history. This history, tarnished with the countless number of tragedies that have befallen the celts in Iberia and the native Americans of Venezuela, from unceded occupation, to indentured servitude, to slavery, to active service in European wars, all for the benefit of the euro-centric elites who continue to occupy their lands. Although arguably, in modern Spain Galicia, Catalonia and the Basque region are politically autonomous regions.

As Robert Patch explains, at "the heart of the colonial economy and colonial system were the indigenous people...incorporated into the world economy through the mechanisms of colonialism" (Patch, 2013: 17). As will be explored in volume two 'A Rake's Progress', these European artificial constructs, over 500 years ago subjugated the mainland and the island peoples who formed part of a centuries old intricate network of native American trading posts of the Cedrosan Saladoid, who are believed to have migrated from the "Orinoco basin via the Lesser Antilles into Puerto Rico and eventually into the Eastern Portion of the Dominican Republic" (Ramos, 2010: 5). This organic spreading out from the Venezuelan mainland, demonstrates how theses native American cultures and First Nations of the Caribbean may have been seeded from the First Nations of Venezuela. Arguably, had the First Nations of Venezuela not been subject to a full-scale military invasion and occupation, they would have continued to thrive on the Mainland and in their Caribbean outposts.

In the next volume, as well as further discussing the invasion and occupation of the lands of these First Nations of Venezuela, we will also be exploring the African cultures, rituals and beliefs that have had a huge impact on Venezuelan culture. Moreover, it could be suggested that even the creation of the Venezuelan Republic and Simon Bolivar's liberation movement was simply another vehicle for the slave-owning, euro-centric Celtic descended elites called the 'Mantuanos', who had historically run and profited from the occupation of Venezuela, to disguise their continued occupation and control with a narrative of freedom and democracy for all.

Bibliography

Patch, R.W., (2013) Indians and the Political Economy of Colonial Central America 1670-1810, Oklahoma: University of Oklahoma Press

Popper, K. R. (2020). The open society and its enemies (Vol. 119). Princeton et al.: Princeton University Press.

Quinn, J. (2018). In search of the Phoenicians. Princeton et al.: Princeton University Press.

Ramos, R. R. (2010). Rethinking Puerto Rican precolonial history. University of Alabama Press.

Tracy, J. (1993) The Rise of Merchant Empires: Long Distance Trade in the Early Modern World, 1350-1750. Cambridge: Cambridge University Press.

Printed in Great Britain
by Amazon